THE OLD TESTAMENT

A Study Guide

COY D. ROPER

CYPRESS
PUBLICATIONS
An Imprint of Heritage Christian University Press

Copyright © 2023 by Coy D. Roper

Cataloging-in-Publication Data

Roper, Coy D. (Coy Dee), 1937-2023

Notes on the Old Testament / by Coy D. Roper

p. cm.

ISBN: 978-1-956811-53-7 (pbk.); 978-1-956811-54-4 (ebook)

1. Bible. Old Testament—Introductions. 2. Bible. Old Testament—Criticism, interpretation, etc. I. Author. II. Title.

221.61—dc20

Library of Congress Control Number: 2023951863

Cover design by Brad McKinnon and Brittany Vander Maas.

All rights reserved.

No part of this book may be reproduced in any form or by any electronic or mechanical means, including information storage and retrieval systems, without written permission from the author, except for the use of brief quotations in a book review.
For information:
Cypress Publications
3625 Helton Drive
PO Box HCU
Florence, AL 35630
www.hcu.edu

To Sharlotte
"I am my beloved's and my beloved is mine."

CONTENTS

Introduction	vii
List of Abbreviations	ix
PART ONE	1
The Christian View of the Old Testament	2
Canon of the Old Testament	5
Twelve Periods of Old Testament History	8
Important Dates in Old Testament History	11
The Ancient Near East	13
PART TWO	14
Introduction to the Pentateuch	15
The Book of Genesis	21
Abraham's Family in Genesis	28
The Book of Exodus	29
The Book of Leviticus	34
Notes on the Holy Days	39
The Book of Numbers	42
History of the Wilderness Wanderings	48
The Book of Deuteronomy	52
Introduction to the Books of History	62
The Book of Joshua	70
The Book of Judges	76
The Book of Ruth	86
The Books of 1 and 2 Samuel	92
The Books of 1 and 2 Kings	99
Notes on the Divided Kingdom	106
The Books of 1 and 2 Chronicles	108
The Book of Ezra	118
The Book of Nehemiah	124
The Book of Esther	130
Introduction to Old Testament Poetry	136
The Book of Job	140
The Book of Psalms	145
Notes on Wisdom Literature	152
The Book of Proverbs	157

The Book of Ecclesiastes	162
The Book of Song of Solomon	166
Introduction to the Books of Prophecy	171
The Message of the Prophets	177
Chronology of the Prophets	182
The Book of Isaiah	186
Notes on the Unity of Isaiah	189
The Book of Jeremiah	196
The Book of Lamentations	201
The Book of Ezekiel	204
The Book of Daniel	208
Overview of the Minor Prophets	212
The Book of Hosea	216
The Book of Joel	220
The Book of Amos	223
The Book of Obadiah	227
The Book of Jonah	230
The Book of Micah	233
The Book of Nahum	236
The Book of Habakkuk	239
The Book of Zephaniah	241
The Book of Haggai	245
The Book of Zechariah	248
The Book of Malachi	252
The Period Between the Testaments	255
PART THREE	258
Works Cited	259
PART FOUR	261
Survey of Approaches to the Study of the Old Testament	262
Preaching from the Old Testament	296
Also by Cypress Publications	303
Heritage Christian University Press	305

INTRODUCTION

Dr. Coy D. Roper was a Renaissance man. Pleasant to the core, he could act, both write and direct plays, sing, lead singing, write, research, teach, preach, and encourage. It would be impossible to judge whether he was easier to admire or to love. If you perceive major positive bias in this introduction, you are correct. Knowing Dr. Roper made me better.

Dr. Roper embodied lifelong learning. As a teacher, he continually improved each of his courses. This was particularly true of his beloved Critical Introduction to the Old Testament. As his *Notes on the Old Testament* continued to grow and deepen, he kept sharing them with his undergraduate students. They treated those notes as treasures.

From the introductory chapters "The Christian View of the Old Testament" and "Canon of the Old Testament" to the concluding essays "Survey of Approaches to the Study of the Old Testament" and "Preaching from the Old Testament," his measured and insightful voice rings clear. He wrote like he spoke—wisely and engagingly.

The heart of *Notes on the Old Testament* is a thoughtful summary of each Old Testament book. Bonus material includes respective introductions to the Pentateuch, the Books of History, Old Testament Poetry, the Wisdom Literature, the Books of Prophecy, and the Period between the Testaments. Each chapter is punctuated with essential resources for further study and deeper understanding. As you read, you'll see hints of the original outline form that has been effectively modified for formatting compatibility. None of the content or power of expression has been lost.

How can one book be appropriate for both a senior-level university course and a work-a-day Christian wanting to improve his or her confidence and competence in handling the Old Testament? I'm not sure. But the beloved Coy Roper somehow accomplished that.

I'm impressed with the book, but even more impressed with the godly man who wrote it.

Bill Bagents

LIST OF ABBREVIATIONS

ANE — Ancient Near East
  DOB — *Dictionary of the Bible*
  DR — David Roper, *A Survey of the Bible Book by Book*
  EHB — *Eerdmans Handbook to the Bible*
  HSB — Harper Study Bible
  ISBE — *International Standard Bible Encyclopedia*
  JB — Jerusalem Bible
  KJV — King James Version
  RSV — Revised Standard Version

PART ONE
INTRODUCTORY MATERIAL

THE CHRISTIAN VIEW OF THE OLD TESTAMENT

OLD TESTAMENT INSPIRED BY GOD

See Hebrews 1:1, 2.

- 2 Timothy 3:16–17 —"All scripture is inspired by God."
- 2 Peter 1:20–21 — "Men moved by the Holy Spirit spoke from God."

OLD TESTAMENT HOLY, UNTOUCHABLE

- It cannot be ignored or broken but must be fulfilled. John 10:35 — "Scripture cannot be broken."

OLD TESTAMENT AUTHORITATIVE

- Since the scriptures were regarded as inspired, profitable, and complete (2 Tim 3:16–17), they were authoritative.

- Since the New Testament writers quote the Old Testament, they show that they accept its authority. See Matthew 19:4; Galatians 4:21–30; Hebrews 1:4–13.

OLD TESTAMENT TESTIFIED OF JESUS

- John 5:39 — "The scriptures ... bear witness of me."
- 1 Peter 1:10–12 — The prophets predicted "the sufferings of Christ and the subsequent glory." See also Acts 8:35.

OLD TESTAMENT FULFILLED BY JESUS

- Matthew 5:17–18 — "I have come ... to fulfill them."
- Luke 24:44 — "Everything written about me in the law of Moses and the prophets and the psalms must be fulfilled."

OLD TESTAMENT SHADOW OF NEW TESTAMENT

- Hebrews 10:1 — "The law has but a shadow of good things to come."

OLD TESTAMENT FAULTY

- Hebrews 8:7 — "If that first covenant had been faultless, there would have been no occasion for a second."
- Hebrews 10:4 — "It is impossible that the blood of bulls and goats should take away sins."

OLD TESTAMENT INFERIOR TO NEW TESTAMENT; NEW TESTAMENT BETTER

- Hebrews 8:6 — Christ's covenant "is better, since it is enacted on better promises." Cf. Hebrews 7:22.

OLD TESTAMENT TAKEN AWAY

- Galatians 3:24–25 — "The law was our custodian … now that faith has come, we are no longer under a custodian."
- Ephesians 2:15 — Christ abolished "in his flesh the law of commandments and ordinances." See also Hebrews 1:1–2; Matthew 17:5.

OLD TESTAMENT VALUABLE FOR STUDY

- Romans 15:4 — "Whatever was written in former days was written for our instruction, that … we might have hope."
- 1 Corinthians 10:11 — "These things happened to them as a warning, but they were written down for our instruction."

CANON OF THE OLD TESTAMENT

ENGLISH OLD TESTAMENT (39)

Law (5)

Genesis, Exodus, Leviticus, Numbers, Deuteronomy

History (12)

Joshua, Judges, Ruth, 1 and 2 Samuel, 1 and 2 Kings, 1 and 2 Chronicles, Ezra, Nehemiah, Esther

Poetry (5)

Job, Psalms, Proverbs, Ecclesiastes, Song of Solomon

Major Prophets (5)

Isaiah, Jeremiah, Lamentations, Ezekiel, Daniel

Minor Prophets (12)

Hosea, Joel, Amos, Obadiah, Jonah, Micah, Nahum, Habakkuk, Zephaniah, Haggai, Zechariah, Malachi

CATHOLIC OLD TESTAMENT (JB) (46)

PENTATEUCH (5)

Genesis, Exodus, Leviticus, Numbers, Deuteronomy

HISTORICAL BOOKS (16)

Joshua, Judges, Ruth, 1 and 2 Samuel, 1 and 2 Kings, 1 and 2 Chronicles, Ezra, Nehemiah, *Tobit,*Judith,* Esther,* 1 and 2 Maccabees**

WISDOM BOOKS (7)

Job, Psalms, Proverbs, Ecclesiastes, Song of Songs, *The Book of Wisdom,* Ecclesiasticus**

PROPHETS (18)

Isaiah, Jeremiah, Lamentations, *Baruch,** Ezekiel, *Daniel,** Hosea, Joel, Amos, Obadiah, Jonah Micah, Nahum, Habakkuk, Zephaniah, Haggai, Zechariah, Malachi

   * These books, in whole or in part, are considered part of the apocrypha.

HEBREW BIBLE (24)

LAW (TORAH) (5)

Genesis, Exodus, Leviticus, Numbers, Deuteronomy

PROPHETS (NABA'IM) (8)
FORMER PROPHETS

Joshua, Judges, 1 and 2 Samuel, 1 and 2 Kings

LATTER PROPHETS

Isaiah, Jeremiah, Ezekiel

THE TWELVE

Hosea, Joel, Amos, Obadiah, Jonah, Micah, Nahum, Habakkuk, Zephaniah, Haggai, Zechariah, Malachi

WRITINGS (KETHUBJM) (11)
Poetry/Wisdom Literature

Job, Psalms, Proverbs

MEGILLOTH TESTAMENT

Ecclesiastes, Song of Solomon, Lamentations, Ruth, Esther

HISTORICAL BOOKS

Daniel, 1 and 2 Chronicles, Ezra/Nehemiah

TWELVE PERIODS OF OLD TESTAMENT HISTORY

PERIOD: BEGINS, ENDS — CHARACTERS, EVENTS — SCRIPTURES —DATES

Antediluvian: Creation to Flood —Adam, Eve, Cain, Abel, Seth; Creation, 1st murder, Fall — Genesis 1–5; 1 Chronicles 1–9

Postdiluvian: Flood to Call of Abraham — Noah, Shem, Ham, Japheth; Flood, Tower of Babel — Genesis 6–11

Patriarchal: Abraham's Call to Move to Egypt — Abraham, Sarah, Hagar, Isaac, Jacob, Esau, Jacob's family, Joseph — Genesis 12–45; Job

Egyptian Sojourn: Move to Egypt to Crossing Red Sea — Joseph, Moses, Pharoah; Birth and Call of Moses, Plagues, Exodus — Genesis 46– Exodus 11

Wilderness Wanderings: Crossing Red Sea to Crossing Jordan — Moses, Aaron, Miriam, Joshua, Caleb; Law at Sinai; Refusal to enter Canaan — Exodus 12–Deuteronomy 34 — Exodus: 1440 or 1200 BC

Conquest of Canaan: From Jordan to Joshua's Death — Joshua, Caleb; Conquest, Division of Land — Joshua

Judges: Joshua's Death to Saul — Judges, Samuel, Hannah, Eli, Ruth, Request for King — Judges 1–1 Samuel 8; Ruth — Saul: 1050–1010 BC

United Kingdom: Saul to Division of Kingdom — Saul, David, Solomon, Samuel, Rehoboam, Jeroboam, Joab, Ishbosheth; Building of Temple — Samuel; Kings; Chronicles; Psalms; Proverbs; Ecclesiastes; Song of Solomon — David: 1010–970 BC; Solomon: 970–931 BC; Division: 931 BC

Divided Kingdom: Division of Kingdom to Destruction of Israel — Elijah, Elisha, Jeroboam I, Ahab, Jezebel; Elijah at Mt Carmel; Assyrian Conflict — Kings; Chronicles; Isaiah; Hosea; Joel; Amos; Jonah; Micah — Destruction of Israel: 721 BC

Judah Alone: End of Israel to Destruction of Jerusalem — Hezekiah, Isaiah, Manasseh, Josiah; Judah saved from Assyria; Babylonian Conflict — Kings; Chronicles; Jeremiah; Ezekiel;

Habukkak; Nahum; Lamentations; Zephaniah — Fall of Jerusalem: 587 BC

Babylonian Captivity: Destruction of Jerusalem to Return — Daniel, Ezekiel, Zerubbabel, Sheshbazzar, Cyrus, Babylonian Rulers; Return — 2 Kings 25; Daniel; Lamentations; Obadiah — First Return: 538 BC

Restoration: Return from Captivity to End of Old Testament — Ezra, Nehemiah, Zerubbabel, Jeshua, Esther, Haggai, Zechariah; Rebuilding Temple & Walls, Reforms, Covenant Renewal — Ezra; Nehemiah; Haggai; Zechariah; Esther; Malachi — Temple Built: 516 BC; Ezra's Return 457 BC; Nehemiah's Return: 445 BC; End Old Testament: 400 BC

IMPORTANT DATES IN OLD TESTAMENT HISTORY[1]

Event—Approximate Date

1. Birth of Abraham — 2166 BC
2. Jacob's migration to Egypt — 1876 BC
3. Birth of Moses — 1527 BC
4. The exodus - early date — 1446 BC
5. The exodus - late date — 1290 BC

United Monarchy

6. Saul — 1050–1010 BC
7. David — 1010–970 BC
8. Solomon — 970–931 BC
9. Temple begun — ca.966 BC

Kingdom of Judah

10. Rehoboam — 931–913 BC
11. Jehoshaphat — 872–848 BC
12. Uzziah — 790–739 BC

13. Hezekiah — 728–697 BC
14. Manasseh — 697–642 BC
15. Josiah — 640–609 BC
16. Fall of Jerusalem — 587 BC

Kingdom of Israel

17. Jeroboam I — 930–910 BC
18. Ahab — 874–853 BC
19. Jehu — 841–814 BC
20. Jeroboam II — 793–753 BC
21. Fall of Samaria — 721 BC

Some of the Prophets

22. Isaiah — 740–680 BC
23. Jeremiah — 726–585 BC
24. Ezekiel — 592–570 BC

Exilic and Post-Exilic Period

25. Daniel — 600–530 BC
26. Second temple rebuilt — 520–516 BC
27. Ezra's return — 457 BC
28. Nehemiah's return — 445 BC

ENDNOTES

[1] All dates are from Archer, Gleason L., Jr., *A Survey of Old Testament Introduction*, rev. ed. (Chicago: Moody Press, 1974), 495–97, which follows the chronology of J. B. Payne's *Outline of Hebrew History*. Dates given in various sources after 1,000 B.C. vary only within a range of about 10 years; before that, there is a much greater range of differences among scholars.

THE ANCIENT NEAR EAST

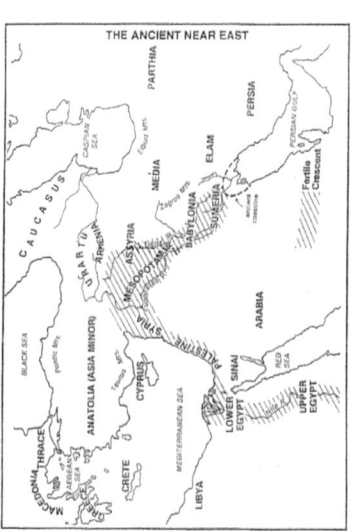

PART TWO
Notes

INTRODUCTION TO THE PENTATEUCH

WHAT IS THE PENTATEUCH?

The Pentateuch consists of the first five books of the Old Testament: Genesis through Deuteronomy. "Pente" means "five." It is a book of five volumes.

It is also called in the English Old Testament "the books of law." Sometimes it is known as the "books of Moses," since these books are attributed to Moses.

In the Hebrew Bible, this portion of scripture is known as the "Torah." Torah is translated "law." Actually, it means "instruction" or "teaching." This is especially appropriate for the Pentateuch since much of it consists of narratives, not laws. But it is all—including the narratives—"Instruction."

WHO WROTE THE PENTATEUCH?

The traditional view, dating at least to the time of Christ or before, is that Moses wrote the Pentateuch. Indeed, the Old Testament and New Testament often quote from the books of the Pentateuch, naming Moses as the author.

However, this question has been a battleground between liberals—who reject the idea that the scriptures are inspired by God—and conservatives—who accept the inspiration of scripture—for more than one hundred years. Liberals believe that the Pentateuch is a compilation made from various sources written at different times and put together by unnamed editors who played a part in the form the final product took. This is called the "documentary hypothesis," since it holds that the Pentateuch is basically derived from four documents:

1. The J document—the earliest, so called because it uses the name "Yahweh" for God.
2. The E document—the next written, uses the name "Elohim" for God.
3. The D document—almost the equivalent of the book of Deuteronomy and dating from the time of Josiah, about 620 BC.
4. The P document—the Priestly document, produced by a priest or a group of priests about the time of the Exile, in the sixth century BC.

The four documents are abbreviated in the following order: JEDP. There are numerous problems with this theory. Among them are the following:

1. It is largely based on guesswork. The fact that scholars do not agree on exactly how many documents there are or to which document particular passages belong indicates that it is a theory that has not and cannot be proved.
2. Specific evidences for the theory—e.g., the alternation of the names of God and the existence of different versions of the same story in a single Bible book—are all questionable.

3. Frequently, the arguments for dividing a passage among various sources are circular. That is, a passage may be assigned to a certain document because it has certain characteristics—e.g., it may use the name *Elohim* for God. However, there may be within the passage evidences which would call the conclusion into question—e.g., within the "E" document, there may be found one or two instances of the use of the name *Yahweh*. When this occurs, the scholars who assigned the passage to "E" will simply say that a later editor (redactor) added the word *Yahweh* to the passage. Thus, the document is to be classified as belonging to "E" because it does not include the name Yahweh, and the inclusion of Yahweh in the passage must be rejected as original because the passage belongs to "E." Such circular reasoning is illogical.
4. Even after one has divided the passage into its various "sources," he is no closer to understanding the passage *as it now reads* in the Bible. He must then go back to the text to try to explain what it means in its own context. Thus, the process of source analysis is not particularly helpful in understanding the Bible as it is. And *the Bible as it is* is the only thing we can be sure of; the existence of sources and their history are purely speculative.

For further information about and refutation of, the documentary theory, see Archer, *A Survey of Old Testament Introduction*.

While the documentary hypothesis need not be accepted, it should also be noted that:

1. Although Moses is frequently spoken of as writing, the Bible nowhere specifically attributes the book of

Genesis to Moses; nor, for that matter, does the Bible clearly attribute the narrative portions of the rest of the Pentateuch to Moses.
2. What happened in Genesis happened before Moses lived.
3. It is possible that the writer of the Pentateuch could have used documents, or written sources, in writing the Pentateuch, and still have been inspired. (See e.g., the book of Luke.)
4. The books of the Pentateuch are themselves anonymous; they do not reveal the names of their author (unlike, e.g., the epistles of Paul).
5. The last chapter of the Pentateuch records the death of Moses.

WHAT DOES THE PENTATEUCH CONTAIN?

Genesis records the primeval history and the beginning of the Hebrew people.

Exodus continues the story of the Hebrew people in Egypt, telling of their deliverance from Egypt (the exodus), of their travel to Sinai, of the giving of the law on Sinai, and of the building of the tabernacle.

Leviticus records many of the other laws that were given on Sinai. It is named after the tribe of Levi, the priestly tribe.

Numbers tells of the journey from Sinai to the border of the promised land, of the failure of the Israelites to enter, of their experiences during their years in the wilderness, and of their return to the borders of Canaan. It is named after two "numberings" or censuses about which the book tells.

Deuteronomy tells of a "second giving" of the law as the Israelites prepared to enter the promised land of Canaan. It largely consists of speeches made by Moses in which he exhorts the Israelites to obey the Law.

HOW IMPORTANT IS THE PENTATEUCH?

It is very important. All of the rest of the Old Testament is based upon it and/or presupposes what it reveals. Three examples will illustrate that point:

1. All the rest of the Old Testament can be seen as the record of God's fulfilling of His promises to Abraham.
2. The deliverance of Israel from Egypt became the one event in Israel's history which, more than any other, defined who Israel was—i.e., the people of God whom He brought out of Egypt "on eagles' wings."
3. The prophets did not claim to be presenting a new law; rather, they claimed to be calling the Israelites back to the Law of Moses.

HOW SHOULD THE PENTATEUCH BE INTERPRETED?

Two special suggestions need to be made regarding the interpretation of the Pentateuch.

First, regarding the narrative sections of the Torah, one should beware of assuming that everything done by the patriarchs—Abraham, Isaac, and Jacob, e.g.—or by the leaders of God's people was approved by God and intended to serve as a good example for saints today. These Old Testament characters were human beings subject to sin, just as people today.

Furthermore, we cannot assume that if the Biblical writer does not condemn an action, then it must be approved. It is not the primary purpose of the Biblical writers in the narrative portions of the Old Testament to preach sermons on faith and godly living; they are telling the story of redemption. As a rule, when the characters in that story do things that are wrong, the writers simply report it as they do other details in the story, without either commending or condemning the deed.

Whether a particular action is right or wrong, whether it can be used as a good example for us or not, will therefore be dependent on other factors—e.g., whether it is used as a good example by an inspired writer, whether it illustrates a desirable attribute which is required elsewhere in scripture, or whether it obviously violates a law of God found elsewhere in scripture.

Second, regarding the legal portions of the Old Testament, we need to understand that while the New Testament teaches that the Old Testament has been taken away, we also need to remember that there is no great difference between the moral and ethical standards of the Law of Moses and those of Christ's covenant. Therefore, even though we are not under the actual regulations found in the Old Testament, we should study the Old Testament laws which lay down those moral and ethical standards with great interest, believing that, in general, they tell us what God still thinks today about morals and ethics.

THE BOOK OF GENESIS
Beginnings

NAME, CLASSIFICATION

The name of the book of Genesis in English is derived from the Septuagint and means "origin" or "beginning." In the Hebrew Bible, the name is similar; it is *Bereshith*. the first word of the book. It means something like: "In the beginning."

Genesis is classified in the English Bible as one of the books of Law and in the Hebrew Bible as one of the books of the Torah (Law).

EMPHASIS

"Beginning" is a very appropriate designation, since the book tells of so many beginnings:

- The beginning of the created universe
- The beginning of life
- The beginning of man
- The beginning of sin
- The beginning of the plan of redemption

- The beginnings of the Hebrew nation
- Etc.

Indeed, the major emphasis of the book of Genesis could be said to be the significant beginnings that relate to the story of God's dealings with man. *Genesis is the book of beginnings.*

AUTHOR

Moses is traditionally regarded as the author of Genesis. However, the book itself does not name its author. Nor is Moses specifically cited as the author of Genesis in the Old Testament or the New Testament. See "Introduction to the Pentateuch." Nevertheless, since the book was regarded as inspired by Jesus and by the writers of the Bible, it is certain that the book was (and thus should be) regarded as inspired.

DATE

If Moses is the author, then the book dates from the time that he lived (which is variously given from about 1450 to 1250 BC). If Moses, or whoever the writer was, used sources in writing the book, then those sources are even older.

HISTORICAL SITUATION

The book begins with the creation, tells of the fall of man, of the flood, and of the call of Abraham. The rest of the book is the story of Abraham's family, with emphases on the line of promise—Abraham, Isaac, Jacob—and on the story of Joseph.

OUTLINE

There are several ways of dividing the book. It can be divided into two major parts:

- The Primeval History — chapters 1–11.
- The Patriarchal History — chapters 12–50.

Then the Patriarchal History can in turn be divided into sections according to the main characters of the division:

- Abraham — chapters 12–23.
- Isaac — chapters 24–26.
- Jacob — chapters 27–36.
- Joseph — chapters 37–50.

It's interesting that the writer of the book provides his own outline by inserting ten times a Hebrew expression including the word *Toledoth*, variously translated as: "the generations of," "the descendants of," or "the history of:"

- 2:4 — The heavens and the earth
- 5:1 — Adam
- 6:9 — Noah
- 10:1 — The sons of Noah
- 11:10 — Shem
- 11:27 — Terah
- 25:12 — Ishmael
- 25:19 — Isaac
- 36:1 — Esau
- 37:2 — The family of Jacob

Obviously, he intended to give the book a structure.

PURPOSE

Judging from the structure found in the book itself, the purpose of the book of Genesis is to show the fulfillment of the promises to Abraham as the solution to the problem of sin. The problem of sin is presented in the "Primeval History." With the story of Abraham, the book's focus shifts from all mankind to the seed of Abraham, as the means by which the problem of sin would be solved. *Genesis shows how God brought forth a people from Abraham's seed through whom all nations would be blessed.*

Thus, there is in Genesis a constant narrowing of the focus of the text: first, Adam; then Seth; then Noah; then Shem; then Abraham. From then on, the book is about how the promises were to be fulfilled—not, for example, through Ishmael, but through Isaac; not through Esau, but through Jacob.

CONTENTS

The history found in Genesis is selective history. The writer is not interested in every detail, but only in that which furthers the Bible story—the story of redemption. While doing so, the book relates significant beginnings.

Genesis tells about the very beginning of the world and of man. Any religion must answer questions about the beginning of all things to the satisfaction of its adherents. Genesis satisfies our need for such answers.

Through the record of the beginning of our world, Genesis establishes the theological foundation for all that follows. The first few chapters tell us of the nature of God, the nature of the universe, and the nature of man.

In the first few chapters, Genesis points out the beginning of the need for redemption. Chapters 1–11 are basically a story of sin and condemnation, even though they also contain examples of

God's saving grace. In these chapters man sins, and then God saves.

In the rest of the book, Genesis demonstrates the beginning of the solution to the problem of sin—how God began to work out His plan of redemption. Thus, in the primeval history, we find the problem presented; in the patriarchal history, we find the beginning of the solution. *Harper Study Bible* says Genesis presents:

- Generation — chapters 1–2.
- Degeneration — chapters 3–11.
- Regeneration — chapters 12–50.

The solution to the problem of sin could be put in terms of the covenant God made with Abraham. God promised:

- a nation
- a land
- a seed through whom all nations would be blessed.

All the rest of the Bible is about how those promises were fulfilled: Genesis 12–50 and the rest of the Pentateuch tells how a nation came into being; Numbers, Deuteronomy, and Joshua tell how that nation obtained a land; and the rest of the Old Testament and the New Testament have to do with the fulfillment of the promise that through Abraham's seed would all nations be blessed.

Genesis also provides background information about other beginnings that were important to the later history of Israel. For instance, Genesis tells where the Edomites came from—they were descended from Esau. It tells us where the Ammonites and Moabites came from—they were descended from Lot. It tells us why Judah (the fourth son of Jacob) became the one through whom the promised seed came, rather than his three older brothers.

Thus, Genesis provides the beginning for the rest of the story of the Bible. Exodus could not be understood without Genesis, but neither for that matter could Matthew or Acts nor the rest of the New Testament.

More specifically, the Bible is put together in such a way that it is obviously one book that tells one story: In the first few chapters of that book, humans lose the right to the tree of life. In the last few chapters, people are granted again the right to the tree of life. In between, we find the record of how God brought about humanity's redemption. Genesis begins that story.

GENESIS AND THE NEW TESTAMENT

The New Testament frequently refers to the characters and incidents of Genesis. See, e.g., Matthew 1:1–3; 3:9; 11:23–24; 19:4–5; 24:37–38; Luke 16:22; 17:28; 1 Timothy 2:13–14; 2 Peter 2:7; John 8:58; Hebrews 11:8.

MEMORABLE PASSAGES

1:1; 1:26; 2:18; 2:24; 3:15; 12:1–3.

DISCUSSION QUESTIONS

1. How should we understand the story of creation? What attempts have been made to harmonize Genesis 1 and 2 with the findings of science?
2. If God didn't want man to sin, why did He place a forbidden tree in the garden? What were the effects of the fall of man? How does Adam's sin relate to the

doctrines of "original sin" and "total hereditary depravity"?
3. What was the "mark" placed on Cain? Why did he fear for his life? Where did he get his wife?
4. Why did the people in Genesis 5 live so long?
5. Was the flood universal or local?
6. Why did God choose Abram, rather than another individual, to be the one through whom He would bless mankind?
7. Abraham was a man of faith, the "father of the faithful." What does that mean? In Abraham's life, what did faith mean or consist of?
8. How does the story of Jacob illustrate that "what a man sows, that shall he reap"?
9. What does the story of Joseph teach about God's providential working?

ABRAHAM'S FAMILY IN GENESIS

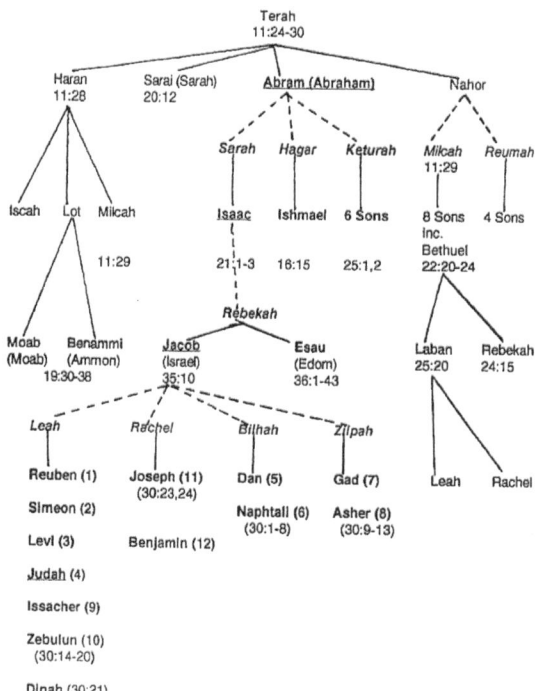

THE BOOK OF EXODUS
Deliverance, Covenant, Law, and Tabernacle

NAME, CLASSIFICATION

In the Hebrew Bible, Exodus is called after the first words of the text and could be translated: "And these are the names." But this —even though it does connect the book to Genesis—does not particularly help us understand what the book is about.

In the English Bible, the name Exodus (derived from the Septuagint) means "departure" or "going out." The book is named after its major event—the departure of the Israelites from Egypt. This does help us understand what the book is about.

In the Old Testament, Exodus is classified as one of the books of Law; in the Hebrew Bible, it is one of the books of the Torah (Law). It is the second book of the Pentateuch.

EMPHASIS

The exodus was the major event in Israelite history, the event which defined Israel as a people especially called and blessed by God. "Exodus" may not, however, be the best way to speak of this event. "Deliverance" would be better, for it makes it clear that Israel's "going out" was not their own doing, but God's. The story of the book doesn't end with Israel's deliverance; it goes on to tell how God made a covenant with Israel and then, as a part of that covenant, gave a law to Israel, which included provisions for their worshiping Him in the tabernacle.

Thus, Exodus describes *how God, in His mercy, delivered Israel, made a covenant with them, gave them His Law, and instructed them to build the tabernacle.*

AUTHOR

According to tradition, the author is Moses. Exodus is closely connected to Genesis in that its story follows, without a break, that which is told in Genesis. The Hebrew begins with the word "and," indicating that the story continues. In fact, the first twelve books of the Old Testament (Genesis through 2 Kings), except for Ruth, tell a continuous story, called by some the "Primary History."

DATE

The main event in the book—the exodus, or deliverance—has been assigned varying dates. The traditional (early) dating places the exodus at about 1440 BC and the entrance into Canaan at about 1400 BC. A more recent (late) dating places the exodus at about 1290 BC and the entrance into Canaan at about 1250 BC. Other dates between these two, and even later, have been suggested by other scholars. There are arguments for and against the early and the late dates.

However, regardless of whether the exodus occurred in the 15th century or the 13th century BC, three things seem clear:

1. The events recorded in the book actually occurred.

2. The events and laws found in the book were almost certainly written down near the time when they occurred or when they were given.
3. The message of the book is the same.

HISTORICAL SITUATION

Exodus begins as Genesis ends, with the family of Jacob (the Israelites) in Egypt. They become so numerous that they are enslaved by the Egyptians. The book then tells how God uses Moses to deliver the people from Egypt and to bring them to Mt. Sinai where God makes a covenant with Israel. The stipulations of the covenant are the laws found in the rest of the book (and in the rest of the Pentateuch), including instructions for building the tabernacle. The book then tells the story of the building of the tabernacle and ends with its completion.

OUTLINE

Basically, the book can be divided into two parts, and the second part can then be divided into two parts:

- Deliverance — chapters 1–18.
- Covenant — chapters 19–40.

1. Covenant and Commandments.
2. Building of the Tabernacle.

PURPOSE

The purpose of the book may be said to be: *To describe how God, in His mercy, delivered Israel, made a covenant with them, and gave them His Law.* The book, therefore, teaches that with redemption comes responsibilities.

The book is also important in that in Exodus 19 we find the covenant that serves as the basis for all of God's dealings with Israel from this point on. God says that Israel will be His people if Israel will do His will. Israel agrees to those terms.

And it is on the basis of this agreement that the rest of the Old Testament is to be understood. Old Testament history demonstrates that as long as Israel kept the covenant by obeying God, then God blessed Israel; when Israel disobeyed, then God turned away from Israel. The Old Testament poets praise the Lord for His grace in condescending to make such a covenant with Israel or lament Israel's failure to keep it. The prophets either urge Israel to keep the covenant or threaten doom because they have not kept it.

EXODUS AND THE REST OF THE BIBLE

The Old Testament in many places refers to the exodus. For example, God refers to Himself as "the Lord your God who brought you up out of the land of Egypt" 125 times in the Old Testament. The New Testament frequently refers to Moses and the exodus. See, e.g., Matthew 17:1–4; John 1:45; Acts 3:22; 1 Corinthians 10:1–12; Hebrews 3:5, 11:23–29.

MEMORABLE PASSAGES

3:5; 5:1a; 19:4–6; 20:2–3.

DISCUSSION QUESTIONS

1. Discuss the date of the exodus.
2. What was the historical situation of Egypt at the time the exodus occurred? Was Egypt a strong nation or a

weak one, compared to other nations of the Ancient Near East (ANE)?

3. In what sense was the Egyptian sojourn good for the people of Israel?
4. What "new" name for God is revealed in Exodus, a name by which He was not known to the Israelites' forefathers? How can this idea be reconciled with the fact that God is called "YAHWEH" in the book of Genesis?
5. Why did God use ten plagues to deliver Israel? Why not just one? What did the plagues accomplish?
6. In what way or ways was the covenant God made with Israel similar to other treaties made between nations or kings in the ANE?
7. What is the relationship between the covenant and God's grace? Is the covenant simply an equal agreement between two parties?
8. There seems to be a covenant made in Exodus 19, and then another covenant is made in Exodus 24. What is the relationship between these two passages?
9. What does each of the Ten Commandments mean? How are the Ten Commandments and the other laws related to the covenant? How may the other laws be related to the Ten Commandments?
10. What relationship does the Law of Moses, given on Sinai and in the rest of the Pentateuch, have to the rest of the Old Testament?

THE BOOK OF LEVITICUS
A Holy Nation

NAME, CLASSIFICATION

In the Hebrew Bible the title comes from the first phrase of the Hebrew text: "And he called." The name of the book of Leviticus in the English Old Testament comes from the Septuagint translators and means "pertaining to the Levites." It suggests that the book is a handbook for priests, who came from the tribe of Levi. (All priests were Levites, but not all Levites were priests since the priests were all descended from Aaron. The Levites who were not priests were their helpers.)

However, the contents of the book might indicate that it was written, not just for the priests, but for the "ordinary" Israelites —to give them instructions as to how they were to worship, etc.

In the English Old Testament, the book is one of the books of Law; in the Hebrew Bible, it is found among the books of the Torah (the Law).

EMPHASIS

The book emphasizes "Holiness." Its theme may be found in Leviticus 11:45: "For I am the Lord who brought you up out of the land of Egypt, to be your God; you shall therefore be holy, for I am holy." The Israelites were called to be "a kingdom of priests and a holy nation." (Exod 19:6) Leviticus shows how God intended to help them become that.

AUTHOR

According to tradition, the author of Leviticus is Moses. Leviticus mostly consists of laws given by God to Israel through Moses.

The liberal view is that Leviticus comes from the "P" (for "Priestly") source and thus dates from the exilic or post-exilic period. The latter part of Leviticus (chs. 17–27) is spoken of as the "Holiness Code." There is no good reason, however, to believe that the material in Leviticus post-dates the time of Moses. In fact, there are parallels to the laws found in Leviticus in other countries of the ANE dating to the time of, or even before, Moses.

DATE

There is no compelling reason to believe that the laws were not recorded at the time they were given. The exodus is sometimes dated about 1440 BC, and sometimes 1290 BC.

HISTORICAL SITUATION

Israel has been delivered out of Egypt and brought to Sinai. There God makes a covenant with the people and gives them His law. As a part of that law, He gives them instructions concerning the building of the tabernacle. The book of Exodus ends with the completion of the tabernacle. Leviticus then contains additional laws given at Sinai during the months that follow. Israel was at Sinai for a year before the people began to move on toward Canaan.

While the book largely consists of legal material, there are two historical sections in Leviticus:

- Leviticus 8–10: The consecration of the priesthood, the first sin offering, historical precedents regarding offerings.
- Leviticus 24:10–23: The case of the cursing of the Lord by a Canaanite.

OUTLINE

HSB gives the following outline:

- The way of approach to a holy God — chapters 1–16.
- The maintaining of fellowship with a holy God — chapters 17–27.

According to this outline, the first part of the book has to do with how one can gain forgiveness and so by grace find a right relationship with God. The second part then deals with how one can maintain that relationship.

PURPOSE

The purpose of the book seems to be to promote holiness in Israel so that Israel might truly be God's "holy nation." This is accomplished by emphasizing:

Holiness. Holiness in Leviticus comes through (*HSB*):

- Sacrifice,
- Proper Ceremony,
- Right Morality.

We need this message about holiness because Christians, too, are called to be holy (1 Pet 1:15). We become holy when we are saved by Christ's sacrifice. As blood was important in the sacrificial system of the Old Testament, so are we saved by blood. (See Lev 17:11.) Then we remain holy by striving to be separate or distinct from the world.

Rituals. Leviticus primarily consists of laws relating to the rituals of the Old Testament religion. Only a small portion of the book consists of narratives. Two topics are dealt with in Leviticus more fully than anywhere else:

- The sacrificial system.
- The system of feasts and festivals.

This emphasis also has some value for the present age. We are inclined to downplay the importance of ritual; almost the only time we use the word we speak of "mere ritual" or "empty rituals." The book of Leviticus should cause us to think again about the value of ritual—not of "mere ritual" or of "empty rituals," but of ritual properly used, including the heartfelt devotion and wholehearted participation of those who are involved in observing it.

LEVITICUS AND THE NEW TESTAMENT

The idea of Christ as the "lamb of God"—the sacrifice for sins—relates to Leviticus. The book of Hebrews has a large number of allusions to, or quotations from, Leviticus. Also, the command to "love your neighbor as yourself" is found in Leviticus and is repeated several times in the New Testament.

MEMORABLE PASSAGES

11:45; 17:11; 19:18.

DISCUSSION QUESTIONS

1. According to the Documentary Hypothesis, when did the "P" document originate? How was it used in the formation of the Pentateuch? What arguments are there against this position?
2. What did, and what does, it mean to be holy? Is "holiness" today, in the Bible sense, largely a matter of how you look or how you talk?
3. "Uncleanness" is a concept encountered frequently in Leviticus. What does it mean? How does the idea of "holiness" relate to the idea of "cleanness"?
4. What kinds of sacrifices were there? What did the sacrifices accomplish—what purpose(s) did they serve? What was required of the worshipers before the sacrifices could be accepted? How do these sacrifices compare to Christ's sacrifice?
5. Discuss the laws of Leviticus 19. How do such laws as these relate to our responsibilities in the Christian age?
6. What blessings and curses are involved in obeying, or failing to obey, the Law?

NOTES ON THE HOLY DAYS

THREE MAJOR FEASTS

Each of these occasions required the participation of all Israelite males at the Sanctuary. These feasts are established in Exodus 23:14, 17; 34:23; Deuteronomy 16:16-17. This format will be used to describe each of these events: Feast, Holy Day — Scripture(s) — Date, Time — Significance, Activities.

Passover (Feast of Unleavened Bread) — Exod 12:1-20; Exod 23:15; Lev 23:5 — Month of Abib/(March–April)/ Early Spring, barley harvest — Remembered deliverance from Egypt.

Feast of Weeks (Harvest, Pentecost) — Exod 23:16; 34:22; Lev 23:15-21; Num 28:26; Acts 2:1 — 50 days later, Late Spring, beginning of wheat harvest — Firstfruits offered to God.

Feast of Ingathering (Tabernacles, Booths) — Exod 23:16; 34:22; Lev 23:33–43; Deut 16:16; Neh 8 — Fall Harvest, Month 7, days 15–22. Tishri (Sept-Oct) — Lived in shelters made from branches; thanksgiving for harvest, remembrance of time in wilderness.

OTHER OLD TESTAMENT HOLY DAYS AND YEARS

Feast of Trumpets — Num 29:1–6; Lev 23:23–25 — Month 7, day 1. Tishri. — Day of rest, extra offerings, Source of New Year Festival: Rosh Hashanah.

Day of Atonement (Yom Kippur) — Lev 16 — Month 7, day 10. Tishri — Confession of, and atonement for, sin; fasting.

New Moon — Isa 1:13; Num 28:11-15; Num 10:10 — Beginning of each lunar month— Special series of sacrifices made. Day of feasting and rest.

Sabbath — Exod 20:1-11; Deut 5:12–15 — Every 7th day — Related to completion of creation, deliverance, rest. No work to be performed.

Sabbatical Year — Lev 25:1–7; Exod 21:2–6; 23:10; Deut 15:1–6, 12–18 — Every 7th year — Land lay fallow; slaves released; debts cancelled.

Jubilee Year — Lev 25:8–34 — Every 50th year — Emphasis: liberty, for land, for property, for slaves.

FEASTS NOT MENTIONED IN THE PENTATEUCH

Feast of Purim — Esther 9 — 14th–15th day of Adar (Feb-March) — Commemorated the deliverance of Jews in Esther's day.

Feast of Dedication (now Hanukkah) — John 10:22 — 25th day of Kislev (December) — Celebrated purification of the temple in 164 BC after its desecration in 168 BC.

THE BOOK OF NUMBERS
In the Wilderness

NAME, CLASSIFICATION

The book's name is derived from the Septuagint and refers to the two censuses, or numberings, in the book. (1:1ff and 26:1ff) The Hebrew title, from the fifth word in the first line of the Hebrew text, is a word that means "in the wilderness." This is a better title for the book since it tells almost all we know of the years Israel spent in the wilderness.

In the English Old Testament, the book is classified among the books of Law; in the Hebrew Bible, it is one of the books of the Torah (Law).

EMPHASIS

Numbers is about the journey of Israel from Sinai to Canaan, a journey that should have taken a few weeks or months at the most, but ended up lasting almost forty years! The book begins with Israel's preparation to leave Sinai but then describes how Israel failed to enter Canaan because of its lack of faith and so was condemned to wander in the wilderness until an entire generation was dead. At the end of the book, a victorious Israel has captured the land east of Jordan and is poised to conquer Canaan—the journey that began at Sinai has ended.

AUTHOR

Like the other books of the Pentateuch, Numbers has traditionally been attributed to Moses.

DATE

The time spent in the wilderness is estimated to have occurred sometime between the fifteenth and thirteenth century BC. If Moses is the author, the date of writing would have been approximately the same as the date of the events.

HISTORICAL SITUATION

The Israelites spent a year at Sinai, receiving the Law and building the tabernacle. Then, at God's command, they journey towards the promised land until they are near enough to send spies in. When the spies return, the people believe the evil "majority report" of the ten spies, rather than believing the "minority report" of Joshua and Caleb, and so are condemned to perish in the wilderness.

They then wander in the wilderness for the next (approximately) thirty-eight years. Near the end of that time, within a year, Miriam (20:1) and Aaron (20:22ff) die.

God then gives Israel instructions to go on towards the promised land. The last year in the wilderness they march again towards Canaan. New leaders are chosen—Eleazar and Joshua. Israel wins great victories over other nations. Reuben, Gad, and a half tribe of Manasseh are settled east of Jordan. At the end of the book, Israel is poised east of Jordan, ready to enter Canaan.

OUTLINE

Archer provides the following outline:

- Preparations for the journey from Sinai — chapters 1:1–10:10.
- From Sinai to Kadesh-Barnea — chapters 10:11–14:45.
- From Kadesh-Barnea to the plains of Moab—chapters 15:1–21:35.
- Encounter with the Moabites and Balaam — chapters 22:1–25:18.
- Preparations for entering Canaan — chapters 26:1–36:13.

CONTENTS, PURPOSE

The book contains both narratives and laws.

The laws were given on various occasions throughout the forty years in the wilderness and are designed to supplement those which are found in Exodus and Leviticus. They may also have served to assure Israel that God will keep His promises and someday allow them to enter the promised land.

The narratives in Numbers stress Israel's sinfulness. Even though the book makes it clear that as Israel prepares to leave Sinai the people are very careful to obey God's instructions, as soon as Israel is in the wilderness, the nation begins to sin (just as they had done when they left Egypt).

The major sin and the most important event in the book has to do with the spies, the unbelief of Israel, and their failure to enter the promised land. See Numbers 13–14. Indeed, all but two (Joshua and Caleb) of the adult males who came out of Egypt died in the wilderness as punishment for this sin. (For a New

Testament application of this incident, see 1 Cor 10 and Heb 3–4.)

Many other sins are recorded as well. In fact, it can be said that *a major emphasis in Numbers is sin with its resultant punishment.* The sins of Israel include the following:

- At Taberah, the people complain and are punished by fire (11:1–3)
- The people want meat. God sends quail, but also sends a plague (11:4–35, v. 33)
- Miriam and Aaron rebel. Leprosy results (12:16)
- Twelve spies are sent out. People die by the plague (13–14, 14:37)
- A man is put to death for breaking the Sabbath (15:32ff)
- Korah, Dathan, Abiram rebel. People are swallowed by the earth. Fire destroys 250 (16)
- People reject Moses and Aaron. Plague sent (6:41) God chooses Aaron (17:1ff)
- Moses sins (20:10ff)
- The people murmur again. God punishes them with serpents (21:4ff; See John 3)
- The people are joined by the Midianites and are slain. (25:1–16; See 1 Cor 10)

However, towards the end of the book (see both the story of the conquest of the nations east of the Jordan and the story of Salaam's blessing of Israel), Israel is again blessed by God.

What then is the book intended to teach? What is its purpose? *From a historical standpoint. it is intended to relate how Israel go from Sinai to Canaan and why that journey takes forty years. From a religious or theological standpoint, the book is designed to demonstrate:*

- The cost of sin—the fact that God always punishes sin.
- The need to rely on God.
- The mercy of God, who, in spite of Israel's constant rebellion, continues to forgive and bless. (See Neh 9:17–23.)

NUMBERS AND THE NEW TESTAMENT

Several things in Numbers are referred to in the New Testament. See John 3:14; 1 Corinthians 10; Hebrews 3–4; 2 Peter 2:15–16; Jude 2:11.

MEMORABLE PASSAGES

6:24–26; 13:30; 14:7–10; 24:17.

DISCUSSION QUESTIONS

1. Discuss the "numberings" in the book. What problem do the large numbers cause? What solutions have been suggested to these problems, both by conservatives and by liberals? In the context of the book, what lesson is the author seeking to teach through these numbers?
2. About when did the exodus, wandering, and conquest occur? What are the issues involved? What arguments have been advanced for various positions by different scholars? What are the Biblical ramifications of each position?
3. Discuss the significance of the fact that the incident in Numbers 13 and 14 is used as an example for Christians in the New Testament.

4. What do we know about the Levites, both from Numbers and from other Old Testament books?
5. Discuss the Balaam story. Why is Balaam, a prophet of Mesopotamia, represented as prophesying in the name of Yahweh?
6. Discuss the structure of the book.

HISTORY OF THE WILDERNESS WANDERINGS

Egypt to Sinai

Exodus 12:37 — Left Egypt, after 430 years (12:30)
Exodus 14:26–31 — Delivered through the sea
Exodus 15:22–25 — In Wilderness of Shur, Bitter waters made sweet
Exodus 16:1ff — 2nd month, 15th day, after leaving Egypt Wilderness of Sin. Manna from heaven
Exodus 16:13ff — Quail provided
Exodus 17:8–13 — Israel overcomes Amalek at Rephidim Aaron and Hur hold up Moses's hands
Exodus 18 — Jethro's visit to Israel; Judicial authority delegated

At Mt. Sinai

Exodus 19 — In 3rd month, came to wilderness of Sinai (19:1) Covenant made (19:1–8)
Exodus 20–23 — Laws given—the "Covenant Code"
Exodus 24:1–8 — Covenant ratified with blood

Exodus 31 — Workmen appointed to build tabernacle
Exodus 32 — Sin: Worship of the golden calf
Exodus 34:30–39:22 — Tabernacle built
Exodus 40:17 — 2nd year, 1st month, 1st day: tabernacle completed; God's glory fills it (40:34)
Leviticus 8–10 — Consecration of the priesthood, offering of sacrifices, Nadab and Abihu's sin
Numbers 1:1–4:48 — 2nd year, 2nd month, 1st day: census taken
Numbers 7:1 — Offerings for the tabernacle after it was set up—from the various tribes
Numbers 10:11,12 — 2nd year, 2nd month, 20th day: people set out from Sinai

Journey from Sinai to Canaan

Numbers 11:1–3 — People complain; are punished
Numbers 11:4–35 — People murmur; God gives them quail; Plague
Numbers 12:1–16 — Miriam and Aaron's rebellion
Numbers 12:16–13:33 — Israel encamps in the wilderness of Paran; spies sent out from there, return to Paran, at Kadesh (13:26), with evil report
Numbers 14:1–20ff — People murmur and God announces they will all die in the wilderness
Numbers 14:39–45 — People go up without God and are defeated by the Amalekites and Canaanites
Numbers 15:32ff — Man killed for breaking the Sabbath
Numbers 16:1–50 — Rebellion and death of Korah, Dathan, and Abiram
Numbers 17:1–12 — God testifies to Moses's and Aaron's right to lead

In the Wilderness for Almost Forty Years

Numbers 20:1 — At Kadesh in the wilderness of Zin, 1st month: Miriam's death
    Numbers 20:2–13 — Water for the people, Moses's sin
    Deuteronomy 1:46 — At Kadesh many days
    Deuteronomy 2:1 — Going into the wilderness, they were "many days" about Mount Seir before God told them to turn northward (Deut 2:2)—38 years from leaving Kadesh-Barnea (Deut 1:46–2:1; Num 20:14ff) to crossing the Brook Zered (Num 21:12)

Journey to Canaan

    Deuteronomy 2:2ff — Command to turn northward, instructions concerning the journey from God
    Numbers 20:14ff — Israel refused passage through Edom
    Numbers 20:22–29 — Israel refused passage through Edom. From Kadesh to Mt. Hor. Aaron died there
    Numbers 21:1–3 — Israel defeats the King of Arad in the Negeb
    Numbers 21:4–9 — People murmur; are bitten by serpents
    Numbers 21:21–35 — Sihon and Og defeated. Israel dwells there (21:31–32)
    Numbers 22–24 — Israel in plains of Moab (22:1), Moab, Midian confronted by Israel. Balak, Balaam
    Numbers 25:1–5 — In Shittim, people intermarry with Moabites; are slain as a result
    Numbers 25:6–16 — Midianite woman slain, Midianites
    Numbers 26:1–51 — Second census taken
    Numbers 27 — The case of Zelophad's daughters, Joshua chosen to succeed Moses
    Numbers 31 — Midianites destroyed
    Numbers 32 — Settlement of some Israelites east of Jordan

Numbers 33:1–40 — Summary of Israel's travels (See 33:38)

Numbers 33:50ff — Israel commanded to drive out the Canaanites

Deuteronomy 3:29 — Israel opposite of Beth-peor. Moses looks at the promised land, but cannot enter (3:27)

Deuteronomy 34 — Moses's death

Entrance into Canaan

Joshua 1–3 — After elaborate preparations, Joshua leads Israel over the Jordan into Canaan

THE BOOK OF DEUTERONOMY
The Second Giving of the Law

NAME, CLASSIFICATION

The name of the book comes from the Septuagint and is derived from two Greek words—*nomos*, which means "law," and *deuteros*, which means "two" or "second." So the meaning of the word is something like "second law," or "second giving of the law." "The Hebrew title, 'These are the words,' is simply the first two Hebrew words in the text." (*HSB*)

Deuteronomy is the fifth book of the Pentateuch, classified as "Law" in the English Old Testament, and "Torah" (or Law) in the Hebrew Bible.

EMPHASIS

There is a great emphasis in the book on "the land." The word "land" is found 187 times in the book (according to the KJV), although not all these occurrences refer to the land of Canaan. About thirty-five times (KJV) the expression "the land which the Lord" has given or has sworn, either to the people addressed or to their fathers, is found, generally followed with an exhortation or a statement concerning Israel's entering into or possessing that land. The expression "possess the land" is found at least eight times. Given the name of the book and the emphasis on "the land," it is possible to say that the book emphasizes: *Living by the law after possessing the land which the Lord has given.*

AUTHOR

As with the other books of the Pentateuch, Deuteronomy is traditionally ascribed to Moses. Since the book largely consists of speeches made by Moses, when it is quoted in the New Testament, it is attributed to him.

As the last chapter tells of his death, it is doubtful that it was written by Moses. Most conservatives believe that this passage was added by some inspired writer—perhaps Joshua—after the death of Moses.

One view has it that Deuteronomy (at least in part) is the book found in the temple that helped produce Josiah's reform about 621 BC (2 Kgs 22-23). The reason why some hold this position is that many of Josiah's reforms—in particular, his attempt to centralize worship in Jerusalem—were based on laws found in the book of Deuteronomy, but not found elsewhere in the Pentateuch.

Some go beyond the belief that the book of Deuteronomy was found then to say that it was written then (rather than dating to the time of Moses), to bring about or further Josiah's reform.

While it may be that Deuteronomy was the book found in the temple at that time, there is no adequate reason to believe it had been only recently written.

DATE

If written (or spoken) by Moses, the book should be dated at about the time of the end of the period spent in the wilderness —sometime perhaps between 1400 and 1250 BC. The alternative liberal view would date to the last half of the 7th century BC.

HISTORICAL SITUATION

Where does Deuteronomy fit in the history of Israel?

After spending a year at Sinai, Israel marched toward Canaan. But because they believed the ten spies' evil report, God punished them by causing them to wander in the wilderness until all the adults counted in the first census, except Joshua and Caleb, were dead. For the next 38 years or so Israel was in the wilderness.

At the end of that time, God gave them their marching orders and they moved again toward the promised land. They conquered nations that stood in their way. Two and a half tribes chose the land east of the Jordan and were told they could settle there if they would help the other nine and one-half tribes by sending over their fighting men to assist in the conquest of the territory on the west of the Jordan.

At the end of Numbers, Israel is poised to invade Canaan. Moses, because of his sin, is not to be allowed to go in. A whole new generation has grown up. It is now necessary to:

- Appoint a new leader to take the place of Moses
- Teach this new generation the laws given by God to Israel
- Apply these laws to the new situations that Israel will experience after they enter Canaan
- Exhort Israel to keep these laws

- Give this new generation an opportunity to renew the covenant that God had made with their fathers at Sinai
- Make some arrangements to ensure that God's laws will continue to be taught and obeyed

The last part of Numbers, the book of Deuteronomy, and the first part of Joshua are designed to meet these needs.

Thus, the book of Deuteronomy pictures Moses gathering about him a new generation and speaking to them these words. Ellison says,

> At the end of Deuteronomy we find Israel, the people of God, at the highest level it was to reach in the Old Testament, however much prophetic voices might foretell infinitely higher attainment in the ages to come. Israel was standing on the brink of God's fulfillment of His promises to give them the land, and they already held Transjordan as an earnest of the fulfillment. All the corrupting links with Egypt had vanished during the forty years of wandering. The law had been expounded in its deeper ethical significance, and so the covenant was renewed (Deut 29:1).

CONTENTS, OUTLINE

Basically, the book of Deuteronomy consists of three speeches made by Moses to Israel.

- Moses's first address. chapters 1–4
- Moses's second address. chapters 5–26
- Moses's third address: provision for the renewal of the covenant. chapters 27–30
- Moses's final words and death. chapters 31–34

In chapter 34 Moses was taken up to Mount Nebo to the top of Pisgah and allowed to see all the promised land, although he was not allowed to enter because of his earlier sin. There he died, at the age of 120, but still strong and active. The Lord buried him and no man knows his grave.

It is also possible to see a "covenant" structure in the book, similar to the treaty-covenants made in the second millennium BC in other ANE countries between a "Great King" and his "Vassal King." The following is adapted from *EHB* (see 194, 198, 199) which provides an outline based on the structure of ANE treaties (the item in parenthesis is found in those covenants, but not in Deuteronomy):

- Introduction, or Preamble — naming the author. Moses is named, but it is understood that the covenant is between God and Israel. Deuteronomy 1:1–5
- Historical prologue. Deuteronomy 1:6–4:49
- Stipulations. Deuteronomy 5:1–26:19
- Curses and blessings. Deuteronomy 27:1–30:20
- Succession arrangements and public reading, or Document Clause. Deuteronomy 31:1–34:5
- (List of gods to witness covenant. Sometimes the covenants in the Old Testament call upon inanimate objects as witnesses, but the gods are never used in this way.)

PURPOSE

The purpose of the book of Deuteronomy is to ensure that the Law is kept after Israel enters the promised land. This is accomplished by:

Applying the law to the new situations that will arise. Before Israel entered Canaan, they were desert wanderers. Afterward, they became city dwellers. New organizations emerged. Some laws anticipate these changed conditions:

- Cities of refuge. See Numbers 39:39ff. These provided refuge for the person who accidentally killed another, not for the first-degree murderer. There were six—three east of the Jordan, and three west.
- Levitical cities. See Numbers 35:1ff. There were to be forty-two of these, besides the six cities of refuge. Levi did not receive a portion of land as did the other tribes when Canaan was divided up. (Joseph's two sons' tribes—Ephraim and Manasseh—each received land.) Instead of land, Levi received cities scattered throughout the land.
- Place of Worship. See Deuteronomy 12. When Israel entered the land, they were to destroy the Canaanite places of worship and to worship at "the place which the Lord your God will choose out of all your tribes to put his name and make his habitation there." (12:5) However, the Israelites would be free to slaughter animals and eat meat wherever they lived (12:15ff; this relaxed a regulation that was in effect in the wilderness).
- Kingship. See Deuteronomy 17:14ff. Since God foresaw that once Israel settled in the land the people would demand a king, He gave these laws.
- Prophets. See Deuteronomy 18:9–22. When Israel entered the land, the nation was not to be guided by the words of diviners, soothsayers, etc., but by the words of the Lord revealed through His prophets. Peter applies Deuteronomy 18:15 to Christ in Acts 3. But probably the first application of these words should be to the system of guidance: the people of

every generation and place were to follow the particular prophet God would raise up for them. There are also instructions as to how to distinguish between true and false prophets. See also Deuteronomy 13:1–5.

- Repetition. In order to encourage Israel to keep the law, many of the laws previously given are repeated. *Davis' Dictionary of the Bible* makes this point: "In Exodus, Leviticus, and Numbers, the legislation is represented as in process of enactment, the occasion or the time when the successive installments were received is commonly stated, and each body of statutes is severally declared to proceed from God. In Deuteronomy, on the other hand, the law is represented, not as being enacted, but as being rehearsed or expounded." (p. 175)
- For instance, the Ten Commandments are repeated in Deuteronomy 5. (See also Exod 20.)
- Emphasizing the need to teach the Law continually. See Deuteronomy 6:4–8. This passage begins with the *Shema*—"Hear, O Israel: The Lord our God is one Lord ..."—a kind of creedal statement at the heart of Old Testament religion, named after the Hebrew word for "hear" with which the clause begins. It then goes on to emphasize how the law was to be passed on from one generation to the next. This was the basic educational system of the Law. Exhortations to obedience. Deuteronomy emphasizes exhortation; thus, it is spoken of as "hortatory" in nature. "Hortatory" means "pertaining to exhortation." In each of Moses's speeches, he exhorts the people to obey. If the people obey, God will bless them. If they disobey, God will curse them, punish them, destroy them. See: 4:1–2;

5:1; 6:1–2; 10:12–13; 11:1; 11:18–23; 12:16–28; 29:29; 30:15–20.
- Provision for the renewal of the covenant. Just as God had made a covenant with those He brought out of Egypt, it was necessary for this new generation to swear allegiance to Him. Thus, in Deuteronomy 27–30 the stage is set for a great covenant renewal ceremony which is to take place after Israel enters Canaan. The people are to stand on Mt. Ebal and Mt. Gerizim. The priests are to spell out the blessings and the curses, and, presumably, the people will have the opportunity to say that they will obey all the words of the Lord, as their fathers did at Sinai. The ceremony itself is not found in Deuteronomy but in Joshua 8:30ff.

DEUTERONOMY AND THE REST OF THE BIBLE

- The instructions regarding the king (Deut 17:14–20) may be contrasted with what actually happened during the days of the United Kingdom, especially during the kingship of Solomon.
- In the New Testament, the command to "love the Lord your God with all your heart." (6:5) is said by Jesus to be the greatest commandment in the law (Matt 22:37, et al.).
- Deuteronomy 18:15, 19 is quoted by Peter in Acts 3:22–23 and applied to Jesus.
- "Based on the United Bible Societies' Greek New Testament, Deuteronomy is quoted or cited 195 times in the New Testament, exceeded only by references to Psalms, Isaiah, Genesis, and Exodus, in that order." (LaSor, footnote 19, p. 188.)

MEMORABLE PASSAGES

6:4–9; 10:12–13; 13:1–3; 18:15, 29; 29:29; 30:11–14.

DISCUSSION QUESTIONS

1. What are the arguments for and against thinking of Deuteronomy as the book found in the temple at the time of Josiah's reformation? Could one believe that theory and still accept the inspiration of Deuteronomy?
2. What was the structure of treaties, or covenants, in the ANE in the second century BC? How does the structure of Deuteronomy generally follow that pattern? What other Old Testament passages generally follow that structure?
3. How can God's command to destroy the nations of the land be reconciled with the nature of God as a God of grace and a good God?
4. Does Deuteronomy 12 necessarily teach that worship must be centralized in Jerusalem? Does this passage make the offering of sacrifice at any other place wrong?
5. Compare the instructions regarding the king in Deuteronomy 17 with the descriptions of David's and Solomon's kingdoms. Are there discrepancies? If there are, how can those discrepancies be accounted for?
6. Discuss how the passages regarding false prophets may be applied today.
7. What blessings and curses are connected with keeping or failing to keep the law (see also Leviticus)? Are these primarily spiritual or material blessings? Do

they apply primarily, or solely, to the nation as a whole, or do they also apply to individual Israelites? Should we expect the blessings mentioned to be provided for us today if we keep God's law, as is apparently taught by those who accept the "health and wealth gospel"?

INTRODUCTION TO THE BOOKS OF HISTORY

WHAT ARE THE BOOKS OF HISTORY?

In the English Old Testament, there are twelve books of history; they begin with Joshua and conclude with Esther. In the Hebrew Bible, these books are variously classified: Joshua, Judges, Samuel, and Kings are classified as the "Former Prophets." Ruth and Esther are found among the "Writings." They are two of five little books called the "Megilloth." Chronicles, Ezra and Nehemiah are also found among the "Writings."

WHAT DO THE BOOKS OF HISTORY CONTAIN?

Joshua provides a record of the period known as the Conquest of Canaan and describes the conquest and the division of the land.

Judges deals with the period of the Judges.

Ruth tells how, during the time of the Judges, a Moabite woman became an ancestress of David.

1 and 2 Samuel describe the end of the period of Judges and the beginning of the United Kingdom. 1 Samuel deals with the kingship of Saul and 2 Samuel is about the kingship of David.

1 and 2 Kings begin with the story of Solomon's kingship, tell of the division of the Kingdom, and narrate the story of the Divided Kingdom and of the Judah Alone period, concluding with the destruction of the Southern Kingdom of Judah.

1 and 2 Chronicles begin with genealogies that reach back to Adam, retell the story of the Kingdom(s) of Israel—although with an emphasis that differs from that found in Samuel/Kings—to the time of the captivity, and conclude with the decree allowing the Jews to return to their own land.

Ezra describes the first return from Babylonian Captivity, the rebuilding of the temple, and the reforms instituted by Ezra.

Nehemiah relates how the walls of Jerusalem were rebuilt and then tells about reforms carried out by Nehemiah and about the renewal of the covenant.

Esther is set in Persia during the period of the Restoration. It tells how a Jewish girl named Esther became queen and later was able to save the Jews from destruction.

WHEN DID THE EVENTS IN THESE BOOKS OCCUR?

The following dates are from Archer (all dates BC):

- Exodus — (early date) 1446; (late date) 1290
- Saul, beginning of his reign — 1050
- David, beginning of his reign — 1010
- Solomon, beginning of his reign — 970
- Division of Kingdom — 930
- Fall of Israel to Assyrians — 721
- Fall of Judah to Babylonians, destruction of Jerusalem and temple, beginning of Babylonian captivity — 587 or 586
- Completion of the rebuilding of temple — 516

- Ezra's return — 457
- Nehemiah's return — 445

HOW DO THE BOOKS OF HISTORY RELATE TO ONE ANOTHER?

There are two parallel, partially overlapping, histories of the Israelites found in these books.

The first is found in the books of Joshua, Judges, Samuel, and Kings, the "Former Prophets" in the Hebrew Bible.

Why were these books called prophets, even though they are obviously history? There are several possibilities:

- They were written by prophets
- They feature prophets as their heroes
- They reflect a "prophetic point of view"
- They were intended to teach—a work commonly done by prophets

These four books form a unit that has often been called the "Deuteronomic History" because it is thought to reflect a "Deuteronomic philosophy of history": "Prosperity is due to obedience to the will of God; adversity is due to disobedience and rebellion against God" (*HSB*). But this seems to be a message taught throughout the Old Testament, not just in these books. *EHB* (205, 206) speaks of this same body of literature as the "prophetic history" and says that the "key themes" of the "prophetic history" are:

- Kingship, especially David's dynasty
- The word of the Lord, especially as it came through prophets
- The temple at Jerusalem
- Worship—the standard against which all kings were judged: "Was the Lord worshipped at Jerusalem in

purity, or were foreign, idolatrous influences allowed to continue? Were high places (the old, pagan shrines) stamped out or allowed to continue?" (EHB 205–206)

These books tell a continuing story ending about 560 BC; the final author must have lived about then. But early materials are included. Various sources, some of which are named, were used in the writing.

The second is found in Chronicles, Ezra, and Nehemiah.

Chronicles retells, in part, the history told in Samuel and Kings. However, there are differences:

1. Since the genealogies that begin 1 Chronicles reach back to the beginning, Chronicles evidently is intended to connect the latest events in Israel's history (and Chronicles is obviously post-exilic) with the earliest history of mankind. It is intended to cover all of history to the author's day.
2. Chronicles also differs in its emphases from Samuel/Kings. Among those differences are the following:

- Chronicles emphasizes genealogies and lists, the temple, the Davidic line, the Levites, and, in general, priestly concerns.
- Chronicles begins at a different point; it says almost nothing about Saul.
- Chronicles virtually ignores the Northern Kingdom of Israel.
- Chronicles ignores the sins of David and Solomon.

Ezra then continues the story where Chronicles leaves it. The last verses of Chronicles are repeated at the beginning of Ezra. And Nehemiah continues the story told in Ezra.

In each of these two (partially) parallel histories can be found a book that does not advance the history of the entire work, but rather tells a story that relates to that period of history: Ruth, which is related to the "Prophetic History;" and Esther, which can be related to the "Chronicler's History."

So from Joshua through Nehemiah can be found the story of the Israelites from the entrance into Canaan to their restoration to the land after the Babylonian Captivity.

WHAT IS THIS HISTORY LIKE?

First, it is selective history. It does not include every detail, but only that information that is necessary to accomplish the purpose(s) of the writer(s). Although different writers and books have different purposes, in general, it may be said that the purpose of this history throughout is religious or theological. It intends to teach something about God and His purposes and plan. Therefore, details that might seem important to someone more interested in political or secular history are omitted and others that might seem unimportant are included.

Perhaps the best example of this can be found in connection with Omri, a king of the Northern Kingdom in the ninth century BC. From records of countries in adjacent lands we know that Omri was considered a powerful and important king. Even a century after his death, Assyria still referred to Israel as the "House of Omri." [Lewis, Jack P., *Historical Backgrounds of Bible History* (Grand Rapids, Ml: Baker Book House, 1971) 94] But the Biblical writer devotes only a few verses to him and his reign (1 Kgs 16:16–28). Why? Because we must conclude, he was an evil king who, from the writer's standpoint, contributed nothing worthwhile to the accomplishment of God's purposes. He was important from a worldly standpoint, but relatively unimportant from the viewpoint of Kings, because its author had a religious purpose.

Is this to say that the history found in these books is somehow deficient—too subjective, or even largely mythical rather than historical? Not at all. In fact, what has been said of Bible history-writing can also be said of any history-writing: It is selective. It must be because not every fact can ever be included in any history. (If it were, it would either not be history—it might be "annals"—or else it would be so detailed as to be unreadable.) And as soon as the principle of "selectivity" is admitted as being involved in writing history, the author's purpose also becomes important, for the author's purpose will always determine what he selects, or includes, in his history. *Thus, the history-writing found in the Bible differs from secular history-writing only in that a different purpose lies behind its selectivity.*

Second, it is reliable history. Since at many points, the Biblical historian's interest does not coincide with that of the modern historian, it is not always possible to verify that the story he tells accords with known historical facts. For example, we should not, as a rule, expect miracles to be verified by ancient historical records. But at those points where Bible history can be checked against known facts, the Bible's historical accounts have again and again proved to be accurate.

Third, it is well-written history, in that:

- In contrast to the annals of contemporary kings of other lands, *it deals with the causes and consequences of events*. Its characters bring grief upon themselves; they are not the victims of "blind fate" or capricious gods; rather, they reap what they sow. And the historical books illustrate that decisions and mistakes can have far-reaching effects.
- In contrast to the bragging accounts of ANE kings (who, it would appear from their own writings, never lost a battle or made a mistake), *this history is forthright*

in reporting the weaknesses of its main characters. Regarding the "heroes" of Israel, the books "tell it like it is;" they picture these great men "warts and all." Even David, the greatest of all Israel's kings, sins! And the writer does not excuse the great king but goes to some length to describe the sin's terrible consequences.

- *It is rich in detail and true to life.* The characters we meet in these books are, for the most part, three-dimensional characters, just as complicated and just as much a mixture of good and bad as people are in "real life." The "good guys" are not all good or always good, and the "bad guys" are not all bad or always bad. Unforgettable portraits are painted of men such as Eli, Samuel, Saul, David, Joab, and Absalom. And in many cases, the narratives are so detailed as to require us to believe that they are reported by an eyewitness.

HOW DO YOU INTERPRET THIS HISTORY?

It is important, first, to remember that the author has a purpose in writing history other than merely to report "the facts." The interpreter's first duty in dealing with a historical book is to try to discover the writer's primary purpose in composing it. The overall purpose must be sought before the purpose of any individual narrative can be properly investigated.

It is important, second, to remember that the main aim of the author will focus on God. The question to ask in interpreting the historical passages is: What is God doing in this incident? This is not to say that the people in the Bible story are unimportant; nor is it to say that God doesn't intend for us to learn from the examples found in the Old Testament (see Heb 11). But it is to say that the primary point of any narrative must be related to what God has done or is doing. For example:

- In the story of Gideon and the Midianites, the most important point is that God gave the people victory.
- In the story of David and Goliath, David is victorious because he relies on God, and Goliath is defeated because he has made light of Israel's God.
- In the story of Ruth, it is God who gives Ruth a child and Naomi a grandchild.
- In the story of Esther, even though the name of God is not used, it is He who saves Israel from destruction as He works through Esther.

It is important, third, to remember that the details of a story may not "mean" anything (may not be significant). The story itself may be intended to teach something to its readers, but the details may be just that—details necessary to tell the story. For example, there is no reason to believe that the fact that David picked up five smooth stones when he went out to meet Goliath has any "deep spiritual meaning." It was simply a fact that was reported.

It is important, fourth, to remember that allegory and analogy are not helpful in interpretation and may be dangerous in application. They do not really help us understand the passage in its own context, and, if we are not careful, when we use allegory and/or analogy to apply Old Testament narratives to present-day concerns, we can end up being guilty of twisting the scriptures (2 Pet 3:16) to make them mean what we want them to mean.

THE BOOK OF JOSHUA
The Conquest of Canaan

NAME, CLASSIFICATION

The book gets its name from its main character, Joshua, whose name means "Yahweh is salvation." ("Jesus" is the Greek form of the Hebrew name "Joshua.") The book of Joshua can almost be thought of as the story of Joshua from the time of the entrance into Canaan to his death.

In the English Old Testament, the book is classified as one of the books of history. In the Hebrew Bible, along with Judges, Samuel, and Kings, the book of Joshua is classified among the "Former Prophets."

These books are frequently called the "Deuteronomic History" because they are thought to reflect the philosophy of history found in Deuteronomy—namely that "prosperity is due to obedience to the will of God; adversity is due to disobedience and rebellion against God." (*HSB*) *EHB*, in contrast, speaks of these same books as the "Prophetic History." They may be thought of as "prophetic," even though they consist mostly of historical material because they:

- reflect a prophetic point of view, and
- are intended to teach.

EMPHASIS

The book emphasizes the fulfillment of the "land promise," made originally to Abraham and then renewed to the people of Israel. It tells how Israel conquered the land and then divided it among themselves. As it concludes, the people renew their covenant with God and Joshua sends "the people away, every man to his inheritance." (Josh 24:28) A new day has dawned in Israelite history: the nation has possessed the land of promise and every family has its own share in that land!

AUTHOR, RELATIONSHIP TO OTHER BOOKS, SOURCES

The author of the book of Joshua is unknown.

The entire body of material known as the former prophets—Joshua/Judges/Samuel/Kings—tells a continuous story, from Israel's entrance into the promised land to its exile from that land. The work shows considerable unity. Therefore, it may be assumed that the entire work as we have it was put together by some author or editor in the 6th century BC. If so, there is no doubt that he used earlier written sources that were contemporary with the events they describe. (See, e.g., Josh 10:13.) We can also be sure that the entire process was overseen by God so that what was written can be spoken of as inspired.

Some connect the book of Joshua with what has gone before, rather than with what comes after, and believe they find in it the same sources found in the Pentateuch. Therefore, they speak of a Hexateuch, rather than a Pentateuch.

DATE

If the books of Joshua, Judges, Samuel, and Kings are thought of as a unit, the final edition of this volume would have been about 560 BC, the date of the latest event recorded in Kings.

The conquest has been variously dated. If the "early date" is accepted, the conquest would have begun about 1400 BC. The *ISBE* suggests 28–30 years for the book of Joshua. *EHB* seems to date the conquest about 1240–1220 BC. For what the book itself says, see 14:7–10; 23:1; 24:29–31. Caleb was 85; he would have been 79 when he entered the land; thus, the conquest took six years. But it appears that a long time passed between the conquest and the death of Joshua, and more time elapsed after the death of Joshua until the beginning of the period of the Judges.

HISTORICAL SITUATION

Moses has died and Joshua has been installed as his successor as leader of all Israel. The nation is ready, forty years after leaving Egypt, to enter into and possess the land of Canaan which God had promised to give them.

The book covers the historical period known as the "Conquest of Canaan" and tells first of Israel's conquest of the land. After elaborate preparations, the people cross the Jordan River on dry ground and set up camp at Gilgal. Next comes the spectacular victory over Jericho. After experiencing a temporary setback at Ai, the people swear allegiance to God at a covenant ceremony (in keeping with instructions given in Deuteronomy) at Mt. Ebal and Mt. Gerizim. Then they make an ill-advised alliance with Gibeon. This in turn triggers the battle in which Joshua leads Israel to victory over an alliance of kings in the south of Canaan. Then Israel triumphs over an alliance of kings in the north. At that point, the land of Canaan as a whole is under Israel's control, although individual cities and territories yet remain to be conquered.

Then the land is divided among the twelve tribes.

Finally, Joshua addresses the people, reminding them of what God had done for them and urging them to be loyal to God. The people respond by vowing that they will be faithful to Yahweh.

Many liberal scholars hold other views of the conquest. Some believe there was no real conquest, but instead, there was something like a "peasants' revolt," in which the people of the various cities of Canaan rebelled against and overthrew their own rulers and then joined in an alliance with Yahwists who had recently come into the land. This supposedly happened over and over again until the entire country was populated with peoples who had accepted the religion of Yahweh. Others believe that there was no one period of conquest, but that several different stories of settlement that occurred, perhaps, centuries apart are combined in the book of Joshua. There are other views as well.

It is important to remember, first, that evidence is lacking to prove any of these ideas, and, second, that the Christian who accepts the Bible as the word of God needs to accept the book at face value.

OUTLINE

The book divides itself into three parts:

- The conquest of Canaan—chapters 1–12
- The division of Canaan—chapters 13–21
- Joshua's final discourses—chapters 22–24

PURPOSE

The purpose of the book of Joshua is to reveal how God, in keeping with His promises to Abraham, kept His promise to give Israel the land of Canaan.

It serves other purposes, too. The book illustrates that at this crucial period in Israel's history, Israel was not left without a leader like Moses; the book is largely about the career of Joshua and frequently suggests parallels between his work and that of Moses. It also demonstrates that the fulfillment of God's promises, though accomplished by God's power, depends on Israel's cooperation. In this regard, it especially shows that Israel cannot be guilty of sin and continue to enjoy God's blessings. In addition, it furthers the Bible story of redemption by narrating how the tribes possessed the promised land. Until the end of the Old Testament, the history of Israel is tied to the history of the land of Palestine.

JOSHUA AND THE NEW TESTAMENT

See Hebrews 4:4; 11:30–31.

MEMORABLE PASSAGES

1:6–8; 24:14–15.

DISCUSSION QUESTIONS

1. Discuss the various views of the conquest. What archaeological data bears on this issue? Could there be any truth in any of the liberal assertions concerning the conquest?

2. Discuss the land promise. Was it a perpetual promise? Did God give the land of Canaan to the Jews in perpetuity, until the end of time? Or was the promise altogether fulfilled when the Israelites, led by Joshua, conquered Canaan?
3. Was the land altogether conquered or only partially conquered? Could both ideas be right?
4. Discuss the idea of "collective guilt" found in the Old Testament. Why would God destroy entire cities, including women and children? Why did Achan's family have to be killed, along with Achan himself?
5. How many similarities can you find between the career of Joshua and that of Moses? What conclusions should we reach from these similarities?
6. Why is it significant that Rahab and the Gibeonites had both heard of Israel's deliverance from Egypt? What else had they heard of?

THE BOOK OF JUDGES
Apostasy, Oppression, and Deliverance

NAME, CLASSIFICATION

The book is named after the major characters of the book—the judges, who were sent by God to deliver Israel from the hand of oppressors. In the English Old Testament, it is classified as a book of history; in the Hebrew Bible, as one of the Former Prophets.

EMPHASIS

The book itself provides a clue to its emphasis in Judges 2:11–23, where it points out that during this period there is a recurring pattern: Israel sins; God is angry with Israel and gives them over to a plunderer; after a while the people cry out under their oppression; then God, moved with pity, raises up a judge to deliver them *from* their oppressor. After the days of the judge, however, they go back into sin, and the cycle starts all over again.

This four-part cycle can be summed up as:

1. Apostasy
2. Oppression
3. Repentance and Renewal
4. Deliverance.

(Or: Sin, Servitude, Supplication, Salvation. Or: Relapse [or Rebellion], Retribution, Repentance [including Regret], Rescue.)

Thus, the book emphasizes that sin brings God's judgment, but repentance results in God's deliverance.

AUTHOR, DATE OF WRITING

No author is named. As a part of the "Deuteronomic History" or "Prophetic History" which includes all the Former Prophets, it continues the story of Joshua and leads into the history told in Samuel. Consequently, it was probably written (or put together in its final form) by the same person and at the same time as the other Former Prophets.

With the other former prophets (Joshua, Samuel, Kings), Judges was probably written long after the events it records, although contemporary sources were certainly used in its composition (the song of Deborah in Judges 5 shows evidence of being a very ancient writing). Since it says over and over that at that time there was no king in Israel (17:6; 18:1; 18:31; 19:1; 21:25), it must have been written when there was (or had been) a king in Israel (Saul became king about 1050 BC). The latest date (since it is the date of the latest event recorded in the prophetic history) it could have been written was about 560 BC.

HISTORICAL SETTING

Israel had been delivered from Egypt, had spent about forty years in the wilderness, and, under Joshua, had conquered the promised land of Canaan. (For notes on the extent of the conquest, see below.)

The land had been divided between the various tribes. Each tribe had the responsibility of driving out the Canaanites who still remained in its land.

These tribes lived apart from one another and, as years passed, apparently grew even further and further apart. Sometimes they fought one another (see Judg 12:1–6 and Judges 20). They even spoke different dialects (see Judg 12:5–6).

There was no king and no central organization. Tribes joined together on occasions against their oppressors, but whether they did so or not was a matter of their own choosing (see Judg 5:17).

What they did have in common was their faith in God, and, apparently, a common allegiance to the sanctuary, which contained the ark of the covenant, located at Shiloh (see Judg 18:31; et al.). This organization is sometimes called, after the model of Greek city-states, an amphictyony. There are, however, probably more differences than similarities between the Greek amphictyony and the Israelite tribes.

The book of Joshua covers the "Conquest of Canaan;" the book of Judges covers the period of "Judges." The events in the book of Ruth also belong to the period of the Judges. (The period of the "Judges" extends into 1 Samuel.) Basically, the book of Judges tells how Israel sinned and was punished by being given over to other nations to be oppressed, and then how God sent judges to deliver the people from those oppressors.

OUTLINE

The book can be divided into three parts:

- Introduction — chapters 1–2.
- The Judges — chapters 3–16.

- The Appendices — chapters 17–21.

THE JUDGES

What were the judges? They were "charismatic leaders," in the sense that they were especially chosen and equipped by God to deliver the people. (Leadership was not hereditary in those days; see the story of Abimelech in Judges 9 for an abortive attempt to make it so.)

What did the judges do? *Their primary function was to serve as deliverers (a military function).* (See Judg 2:16; 3:15.) In addition, some of them had various *secondary functions*:

- Administrative functions. They were leaders of the people (in a capacity somewhat like that of Moses and Joshua). But there is no evidence that some—such as Samson—led others. Samson seemed to battle the Philistines, Israel's oppressors, all by himself. (See also Shamgar—3:31.) In contrast, this may have been the primary function of some, who are not said to have delivered Israel from anyone: see Tola, 10:1; Jair, 10:3; Ibzan, 12:8; Elon, 12:11; Abdon, 12:13.
- Judicial functions. Also, it appears that they were (or became) judges of legal matters. See 1 Samuel 6:15–17.
- Religious functions. They may also have been religious leaders—Deborah was a prophetess (Judg 4:4); Gideon destroyed idols (Judg 6:25ff). The fact that the book says that after their death the people turned to Baals may imply that they were religious leaders (see Judg 8:33ff).

Who were they, and from whom did they deliver Israel? The following information, for the most part, comes from *EHB*;

notice that there is a considerable difference in the amount of information given about various judges. Also, it should be remembered that Eli (1 Sam 4:18) and Samuel (1 Sam 7:15) are spoken of as judging Israel; Abimelech is not spoken of as a judge of Israel, but he is said to have "ruled Israel" (Judg 9:22).

Judge — Oppressor — App. Date — Interesting Fact

1. Othniel of Judah (3:9) — Cushan-rishathaim — 1200 BC
2. Ehud of Benjamin (3:15) — Eglon of Moab — 1170 BC — Left-handed assassin
3. Shamgar (3:31) — Philistines — 1150 BC — Killed 600 Philistines with an oxgoad
4. Deborah (Ephraim) and Barak (Naphtali) — Jabin and Sisera of Canaan — 1125 BC — Deborah a prophetess. (4:4–6)
5. Gideon of Manasseh (6:11) — Midianites and Amalekites — 1100 BC — Won with 300 men
6. Tola of Issachar (10:1)
7. Jair of Gilead (10:3) — Had 30 sons who rode on 30 donkeys
8. Jephthah of Gilead (11:11) — Ammonites — 1070 BC — Converted thief who offered his daughter
9. Ibzan of Bethlehem (12:8) — Had 30 sons and 30 daughters
10. Elon of Zebulun (12:11)
11. Abdon of Ephraim (12:13) — Had 40 sons and 30 grandsons
12. Samson of Dan (15:20) — Philistines — 1070 BC — Strong man, married to Delilah; he killed more Philistines in death than in life

THE APPENDICES

Chapters 17–21 are frequently called appendices because they appear to be different from, and unnecessary to the primary narrative of the book of Judges. They tell several interesting, but not—apparently—very edifying stories. Why are they included? Here are some possibilities:

- To illustrate the depths to which Israel had sunk during this period—which could, in part, be said to be the consequences of being without a king
- To show how one tribe on one occasion escaped destruction.
- To give a partial history of a certain part of Israel, a part which became increasingly important in later years—the hill country of Ephraim
- To show how Israel acted together on at least one occasion, thus paving the way for the uniting of the tribes in one kingdom

PURPOSES

The period of the judges may be thought of as "The Dark Age" of Israel's history. There was little, if anything, to lighten the picture.

- *Politically, Israel was weak.* The refrain "there was no king in Israel" implies a time of near-chaos, anarchy, and political weakness. Israel was easy prey to all its enemies. There was internal weakness, involving fighting between the tribes (see Judg 12:1–6; Judg 18 and 19; Judg 20 and 21). There was an attempted takeover of the kingship by force (see Judg 9). There were "fightings within and foes without."

- *Religiously, Israel was unfaithful to God.* There was constantly recurring apostasy with resultant punishment. There were serious religious irregularities (Judg 6:25ff; 8:22–27;17:1–6) and terrible sins (see Judg 19).

Why did Israel experience these problems during this period?

- *Disobedience.* Much of the trouble is blamed on the Israelites' failure to subdue the land completely, even though they had been commanded to drive out the previous inhabitants. See 1:19, 21, 27, 29, 30, 31, 32, 33, 34, 35; 2:1–23; 3:5, 6. This resulted in the Israelites' intermarrying with the people of the land and then in their becoming worshipers of other gods.
- *Forgetfulness.* There was also failure to follow their faithful fathers. See 2:7, 10.
- *Lawlessness.* And the people refused to submit to any higher authority. Anarchy reigned. See 17:6 and 20:25.

What purpose, or purposes, then did the book serve? *Its main purpose must be to teach the lesson of all the "prophetic history" or "Deuteronomic history": If we obey God, we will be blessed: if we disobey, we will be cursed.*
In addition to that:

- Judges gives the history of a transitional period in Israel's history: from the time of the exodus and conquest to the beginning of the story of the United Kingdom.
- It teaches the lesson that the people of God must depend on God for success. Gideon with three

hundred men can win. Samson with God on his side is more powerful than all the Philistines. Yet man must do his part—see 7:21.
- It teaches that because of God's great mercy, repentance brings deliverance (10:10–16).
- It points out that turning away from God leads to lower and lower depths.
- It illustrates that God raises up "men of the hour"—and He often uses very imperfect men—to accomplish His purposes.

PROBLEMS

Several problems arise in connection with the interpretation of the book of Judges.

1. How much of the land was conquered in the conquest of Canaan? Some passages seem to suggest that every part of Canaan had been subdued by the forces of Israel led by Joshua. See Joshua 11:16–12:24; 21:43–45; 23:14; 24:13; 24:18.

But other passages make it plain that much of the land, and a number of different peoples, were left unconquered. See Joshua 13:1–6; 13:13; 15:63; 17:12–13; 23:9–13; and Judges 1, especially verses 27ff. (Jerusalem, for instance, was not finally subdued until the time of David; see Josh 15:63; Judg 1:8; 2 Sam 5:6–9.) There is some evidence that Israel particularly occupied the hill country. See Joshua 17:16–18; Judges 1:19; Judges 1:34; 1 Samuel 13:19–22; 1 Kings 20:23.

Can it be true that Israel conquered all the land, but at the same time much was left unconquered? Yes, in that the land as a whole had been subdued, but there were many "pockets of resistance" left to be subdued in "mopping-up operations." Each tribe had the responsibility of completing the subjugation of the land it occupied. That involved completely driving out the people of that land.

2. How long did the period of the Judges last? If all the time indications in the book of Judges are added together, one gets about 390 years. Most students of the Old Testament agree that this era could not have lasted that long. How can this problem in chronology be solved?

It appears that some or most of the judges were sectional rulers or deliverers, rather than rulers or deliverers of all Israel. *EHB* notes: "We know, for example, from 10:7 that the Ammonite oppression in the east and the Philistine oppression in the west occurred at the same time." Thus, it is probable that at least some of the judges served at the same time in different areas of the land and that their "judgeships" overlapped.

3. How can the moral lapses of the judges be explained? This period was a time of great immorality. See Judges 4:17–22. And the judges, God's chosen rulers, were not immune from this general tendency.

- Ehud was an assassin who lied (Judg 3:15–23)
- Gideon had a concubine (Judg 8:31)
- Gideon made an ephod which became the object of idolatry (Judg 8:24–27)
- Abimelech (who, however, does not have God's approval) murders his seventy brothers (Judg 9:5)
- Jephthah was a thief (Judg 11:3)
- Jephthah apparently offered his daughter as a sacrifice (Judg 11:30ff)
- Samson was a womanizer, who seems to have been concerned only about his fleshly desires (Judg 14ff)

Yet some of the judges are pointed to as heroes of faith in Hebrews 11. How can they be examples of faith when they were immoral? *They are examples of faith in that God won victories through them.* For all their moral inadequacies, they were, at the time that they delivered Israel, people firmly committed to the one true God, trusting in Him for His help; thus, they conquered. In this (alone?) they are good examples for us.

MEMORABLE VERSES

7:2; 7:20–21; 18:1.

DISCUSSION QUESTIONS

1. Discuss how the land could have been said to be completely conquered and yet portions of it remain unconquered.
2. Discuss the chronology of the judges. Is it likely that all of the judges ruled over or delivered all Israel—all of the tribes?
3. Discuss how the judges—e.g., Jephthah and Samson—could be thought of as "heroes of faith" in the New Testament (see Heb 11) and still have been guilty of so many shortcomings and sins.
4. Discuss the incident in which Jephthah apparently sacrificed his daughter.
5. What were the original readers supposed to learn from the last few chapters of Judges (the appendices)? What can we learn from them?
6. What does the "Shibboleth" incident (Judg 12) suggest about the relations between the tribes?
7. "There was no king in Israel." Is this absolutely true? Discuss kingship in Israel during the period of the judges.

THE BOOK OF RUTH
A Moabite Ancestress of David

NAME, CLASSIFICATION

The book is named after a Moabite woman who became the great-grandmother of David and who is found in the New Testament genealogy of Christ (Matt 1:5). In the English Bible, Ruth is classified as one of the books of history. But in the Hebrew Bible, it is one of the writings, the "Hagiographa." Within that broader group, it is included among the Megilloth, a group of five little books, each of which is read on a particular feast day.

Apparently, the book was placed after Judges in the Septuagint, and the English versions which follow it, because its action occurs during the time of the judges.

EMPHASIS

There is an emphasis in the book on the fact that Ruth, who would have been well-known to the first readers, was a Moabite. Thus, it was meant to explain how it happened that a Moabite woman became an ancestress of David (in spite of the fact that the

Moabites had often been enemies of Israel) and, more generally, to challenge the notion that there was and could be nothing good about the Gentiles.

AUTHOR, DATE

The author is unknown. The story must be dated during the period of the Judges, perhaps about 1100 BC. But the date of the writing is later, at the earliest sometime during or after the reign of David.

OUTLINE

The book is a narrative that can be divided into

- How Ruth came to Bethlehem — chapter 1
- How Ruth met and attracted Boaz — chapter 2
- How Boaz decided to marry Ruth— chapter 3
- How Boaz and Ruth were married and had a child —chapter 4

HISTORICAL SETTING

At the time of the judges, Elimelech, an Israelite, takes his wife Naomi and his two sons Mahlon and Chilion to Moab to live because of a famine in Israel. The two sons marry Moabite women. Then Elimelech and the two sons die. Naomi determines to return to Israel. One of her daughters-in-law, Ruth, pledges her love to her mother-in-law and returns with her.

They return to Bethlehem, Elimelech's home, and there the two widows live a frugal life. Ruth cares for Naomi by gleaning in the field of a man named Boaz, who is kin to Elimelech's family.

Eventually, after Naomi has encouraged Ruth to let Boaz

know that she would be willing to marry him, Boaz decides to marry Ruth and buys the right to do so from another man, who is a nearer kinsman than he.

So Ruth and Boaz marry, and have a child, Obed, thus making Naomi happy. This child becomes an ancestor of David, and ultimately of Jesus. Bethlehem, Elimelech's and Boaz's town, later becomes known as the "city of David."

VALUE, PURPOSE

The book is in the Bible for the religious purpose(s) it serves. But it has great value in other ways as well.

Literary value. The book displays great literary artistry. This is a marvelous short story. Its central character seems to be Naomi since the story begins and ends with her. Its conflict arises, not from any character within the story, but from the adverse circumstances in which Naomi finds herself; it could be called "Naomi versus the cruelties of life." Its plot has to do with Naomi's losing all that she has—husband, children and heirs, support, land, home—and then regaining it. She regains her home and friends when she returns to Bethlehem. She finds support when Ruth goes out to glean for her. Eventually, she, in a sense, has a child when Ruth is married and bears Obed. See Ruth 4:14–15. So the story ends happily.

Historical value. (1) We learn something about the period of the judges. Although we have spoken of that period as the "Dark Age" of the Israelite nation, and even though it was a time of bloodshed and war, it was also a time when individual families could lead quiet and peaceful lives, concerned only about those matters out of which the fabric of everyday life is woven—love and death, survival, marriage, birth.

(2) We learn something about the customs of that era:

- gleaning (see Deut 24:19)
- levirate marriage (see Ruth 1:11 and Deut 25:5-6)
- other customs—see 3:9 and 4:1 and 4:7

Religious value. Why is Ruth in the Bible? Besides telling us about David's ancestry:

- *The book provides an argument against ethnic prejudice.* Goodness is not limited to Israel; Ruth is also a good, hard-working, benevolent, faithful woman. Furthermore, she becomes a worshiper of Yahweh when she "pledges allegiance" to God, saying to Naomi: "Your God shall be my God." Moabites, and other Gentiles, are acceptable if they accept Yahweh as their God. See Ruth 2:10-12.
- *The book recommends to us godly virtues,* especially as exemplified in the relationship between Ruth and Naomi, and demonstrates that virtue is rewarded. It may be intended to say: "If you are faithful to your pledge, look after your parents, and work hard, then you are likely to be rewarded as Ruth was."
- *The book illustrates how God works providentially to accomplish His will.* Ruth 2:3 says, "And she *happened* to come to the part of the field belonging to Boaz." (Emphasis added.) Was that just a "happenstance," a coincidence? The writer and early readers would not have thought so. Naomi didn't think so. (Ruth 2:20.) The first readers would have believed God brought about that "coincidence" and would have praised God because He worked through all the circumstances of the story to provide childless Naomi with a grandchild. They would also have noticed that God gave her more than He took from her, for that

grandson became the grandfather of David, the greatest of Israel's kings!

The purpose of the book then, beyond telling the facts of David's ancestry, may be said to be to demonstrate that God can work in the adverse circumstances of life to bring triumph out of tragedy.

RUTH AND THE NEW TESTAMENT

Ruth is included in the ancestry of Jesus (see above).

MEMORABLE VERSES

1:16–17; 2:12.

DISCUSSION QUESTIONS

1. Some have thought that the book of Ruth was written with a missionary purpose in mind: to encourage the Jews to seek to convert Gentiles. Some have even seen in it a message written during the fifth century BC as an argument against the exclusiveness of Ezra and Nehemiah. Are these views correct? Might Ruth have something to do with a missionary emphasis in Judaism? When was the book written? Discuss these issues.
2. What restrictions did the Law place on marrying the people of Moab? Does the action of Ruth represent a breach of this law?
3. Explain: (A) Levirate marriage. Why is the practice called by that name? (B) Gleaning. (C) The custom found in Ruth 3:1–13. (D) Why did Boaz's kinsman refuse to buy the field if he also had to marry Ruth?

4. Ruth is sometimes called a love story. Do you think it is? Why or why not?
5. Discuss the fact that the story is set in the period of the judges, and yet the people of Bethlehem seem to be living quiet lives, far from the anarchy, confusion, and wars that we read about in the book of Judges.

THE BOOKS OF 1 AND 2 SAMUEL
Saul and David

NAME, CLASSIFICATION

Originally 1 and 2 Samuel were one book; they tell a continuous story. The Septuagint translators divided the books of Samuel and Kings in the Hebrew Bible into four books and named them "Books of Kingdoms." Jerome in the Latin Vulgate followed the Septuagint, but changed the name to "Books of Kings." The English translations have retained the division into four books, but have also retained the names of the books from the Hebrew Bible; thus we have 1 and 2 Samuel and 1 and 2 Kings.

The book is named after Samuel, an outstanding leader of Israel: a judge, a prophet, and apparently a priest. Though not a king, he was a king-maker—the one whom God chose to anoint the first two kings of Israel. In contrast to the kings, his character was unblemished (1 Sam 12).

In the English Old Testament, 1 and 2 Samuel are classified as books of history. In the Hebrew Bible, Samuel is one of the Former Prophets, along with Joshua, Judges, and Kings.

EMPHASIS

The book is primarily about David's kingship. 1 Samuel begins with the birth and career of Samuel, whose story prepares the reader for the institution of the kingdom. Then it continues with Saul's kingdom, but almost as quickly as Saul is accepted as king, he sins and is rejected by God. Next, in 1 Samuel 16, David is anointed by Samuel, and from that point until the end of 1 Samuel, the focus of the book is on David. The first fifteen chapters of 1 Samuel appear to be a preface to give the reader the background he needs to understand David's story.

AUTHOR, DATE

A Jewish tradition attributed the book to Samuel, but since 1 Samuel 25:1 records his death, he could not have been the author. Therefore, the author is unknown.

Samuel is part of the Former Prophets; as a body of literature (sometimes called the "Deuteronomic History" or the "Prophetic History"), these books could not have been completed before the last event spoken of in them: Jehoiachin's release from prison in Babylon about 560 BC (2 Kgs 25:27–30). The author of the book probably made use of very old sources, at least some of which were contemporary with the events recorded. Scholars speculate that one such source was "The Court History of David" (2 Sam 9–20). From 1 Samuel 9:9, it would appear that the author wrote some time after the events he recorded occurred.

HISTORICAL SITUATION

In general, the two books of Samuel relate the history of the first two kings of the United Kingdom—Saul and David.

To be more precise, 1 Samuel is set during the last part of the period of the Judges and the period of the United Kingdom; 2 Samuel in its entirety is set during the period of the United Kingdom.

The Judges. During this period, which includes 1 Samuel 1-10, the tribes of Israel were bound together primarily by their common faith and allegiance to Yahweh. They also shared a common place of worship—the shrine containing the ark at Shiloh.

1 Samuel records how Samuel was born, why he was brought up at Shiloh by Eli, and how he became a prophet and (leader of the people) who were in a suitable position to anoint the first two kings.

The United Kingdom. The most significant event in these books is the decision of Israel to have a king (1 Sam 8). Although God said that in asking for a king, they were rejecting Him, He had Samuel anoint Saul as the first king of the United Kingdom.

Saul was a transitional figure between the judges and the later kings. He apparently didn't live in an elaborate court or establish a bureaucracy as did David and Solomon. He soon sinned, with the result that God chose David to be king.

David's life was filled with trouble. 1 Samuel records that he spent years trying to avoid Saul's jealous, murderous rage; then, after Saul's death, he spent years contending with Saul's son Ishbosheth before he was accepted as king over all of Israel.

After that, he experienced a relatively short time of triumph and tranquility before he himself sinned. As a consequence, his life was again filled with grief originating from within his own family. 2 Samuel ends with David guilty of another sin—numbering the people—and seeking to atone for that sin by offering sacrifice.

But an event of great spiritual significance occurred when David sought to build a temple. God refused the offer—the task was left to Solomon, but promised David that He would establish his kingdom forever. This gracious promise took its place alongside the promises to Abraham and Moses as the foremost indicators that one day God would send a Messiah, an "anointed one," a Christ.

The story of the United Kingdom continues in 1 Kings 1–12, which tells about Solomon's kingship and then about the division of the kingdom.

The United Kingdom lasted about 120 years. During that time, especially during the reigns of David and Solomon, Israel attained its greatest political and material glory. This was achieved, in part, because the period was a time of relative weakness on the part of the major powers of the ANE.

OUTLINE

Following is a brief summary of the contents of the two books:

- 1 Samuel: Samuel's birth through Saul's death.
- 2 Samuel: Saul's death through the end of David's reign.

A more detailed outline (from *HSB*) might be:
1. Outline of First Samuel:

- The judgeship of Samuel —chapters 1:1–7:17.
- The reign of Saul — chapters 8:1–31:13.

2. Outline of Second Samuel:

- David enters into his kingship — chapters 1:1–4:12.
- The consolidation of David's kingship — chapters 5:1–10:19.
- The sin of David — chapters 11:1–12:31.
- David's troubles — chapters 13:1–18:33.

- David restored to his kingdom — chapters 19:1–20:26.
- The later years of David's kingdom — chapters 21:1 – 24:25.

PURPOSE

The prophetic history (Joshua/Judges/Samuel/Kings) begins with Israel's entrance into the promised land and concludes with the destruction of the kingdom and Judah's deportation to Babylon. One way to look at that history is to see in it the history of the kingdom from planting to full flower to decay and destruction. From that standpoint, the story of David, told in Samuel, coming as it does near the middle of the story (with forty-five chapters before and forty-seven chapters after), represents the full flowering of that kingdom and the climax of the story.

However, the emphasis in Samuel is not on the glory of David's kingdom, although his power, might, and achievements receive considerable attention. Rather, from the standpoint of the space allotted to the stories, the emphasis is on the consequences of, first, Saul's sin, and, second, David's sin. And those consequences, which often affected the people negatively, were themselves the result of Israel's fateful decision to insist upon having a king.

But in the middle of the story stands one important promise: a promise to David that his descendant would build God a house—a temple—and that David's kingdom would be perpetuated "for ever" through this descendant's line. That promise determined, to a great extent, the history of Judah for the next four hundred years and continued to fuel Israel's greatest hopes until the time of Christ.

Perhaps we can say, therefore, that the major purpose of the writer of Samuel is to show the harmful effects of Israel's

decision to replace God as king with an earthly king, by demonstrating the consequences of the kings' sins, while at the same time holding out hope for the future based on God's gracious promise to David.

THE BOOKS OF SAMUEL AND THE NEW TESTAMENT

Jesus is said to be the one descended from David who sits on David's throne—Matthew 1:17; Luke 1:32–33; Acts 2:25–31, 34–36; Romans 1:3; Revelation 5:5.

MEMORABLE PASSAGES

1 Samuel 15:22; 16:7; 17:45; 24:17–19; 30:24; 2 Samuel 7:11–13, 16; 12:7, 13; 18:32–33; 24:24.

DISCUSSION QUESTIONS

1. David was a remarkable, complicated, multi-talented individual. Describe him and discuss his characteristics.
2. How could David be "a man after God's own heart" and still be a sinner?
3. When and how was 2 Samuel 7:12ff fulfilled, or when will it be fulfilled?
4. Discuss the history-writing found in Samuel. Are there indications that the writer was a reliable historian? What are the views of liberal scholars concerning the history of these two books? Why should their views be accepted or rejected? What good can be said about the history-writing in Samuel?
5. What is (are) the view(s) of kingship in Samuel? Is there a contradiction in saying that God didn't want

Israel to have a king, since He says they were rejecting Him as king, and at the same time saying that God allowed them to have a king? How can these two ideas be reconciled?

6. What similarities are there between the reigns of the three kings of the United Kingdom? Do these similarities seem to be intentional? If so, what is the writer trying to teach by pointing them out?

7. Discuss the expression from 1 Samuel 10:10: "And the spirit of God came mightily upon him …"

THE BOOKS OF 1 AND 2 KINGS
The Decline and Fall of Israel's Kingdoms

NAME, CLASSIFICATION

1 and 2 Kings were originally a single book named Kings in the Hebrew Bible. The name "Kings" derives from the fact that these books give the history of the "Kings"—and the Kingdoms —of Israel.

In the English Old Testament, these books are classified as books of History; in the Hebrew Bible, they are together considered one of the "Former Prophets."

EMPHASIS

While Kings is well named in that it gives the history of the kings, and especially the history of the kings after David, it is not primarily interested in "just the (historical) facts." Rather, the writer is concerned about whether each of the kings was righteous or evil. Over and over it states concerning individual kings: "He did what was evil in the sight of the Lord." The consequences of evil-doing are also usually specified. *The book emphasizes, therefore, the moral or spiritual history of the later period of the kingdom(s) of Israel.*

AUTHOR, DATE

According to *HSB*, "Jewish tradition attributed the books to Jeremiah," but "this cannot be verified." The name of the author remains unknown. As the last of the Former Prophets, Kings must have been written by someone who lived about 560 BC, soon after the time when Jehoiachin was freed from prison in Babylon (2 Kgs 25:27). The author undoubtedly used early source materials in his writing (e.g., "the book of the Acts of Solomon," "the book of the Chronicles of the Kings of Judah," and "the book of the Chronicles of the Kings of Israel").

HISTORICAL SETTING

The United Kingdom, during which Israel was ruled by Saul, David, and Solomon, lasted only about 120 years. The history of the first two kings is narrated in 1 and 2 Samuel, but the story of Solomon is told in Kings.

Kings begins with the end of David's reign and the accession of Solomon. Solomon's reign is notable for his wisdom and wealth and, especially, for his construction of the Temple. However, the narrative of Solomon's kingship ends on an unhappy note with his being led into idolatry by the many foreign wives he married. As a consequence, God decrees that the kingdom will be divided after Solomon's death. (1 Kgs 11:11–13)

In fulfillment of that prediction, Rehoboam, his successor, is approached by leaders of the northern tribes asking for a reduction in taxes. Rehoboam refuses, with the result that the northern tribes rebel and make Jeroboam their king. (1 Kgs 12)

Thus, the kingdom is divided into two parts. The Southern

Kingdom, consisting primarily of the tribe of Judah, is known as Judah; the Northern Kingdom, consisting of ten tribes, is called Israel.

Kings then relates the history of these kingdoms. It tells how the Northern Kingdom was destroyed by Assyria about 722 BC. The Southern Kingdom, Judah, continued to exist by itself (hence the name for the period: "Judah Alone") for almost another 140 years until it was destroyed and its people were taken into captivity by the Babylonians. With the destruction of Judah and the deportation of its inhabitants, Kings ends.

The stories of the book of Daniel have their setting in Babylon during the captivity, and Ezra/Nehemiah tells how the people of Judah returned to their own land several decades later.

STYLE

The style of the chapters that deal with the Divided Kingdom has several features that cause it to differ from the other historical books.

1. Unlike Chronicles, it provides a history of both kingdoms, alternating from one to the other, and, in fact, uses considerably more space to tell about the Northern Kingdom than the Southern.

2. Unlike Samuel, it evaluates the kings, stating clearly whether they are good or bad. This evaluation of each is not based on his political or military successes but on his religious loyalty. In addition, it is part of a pattern followed in telling the story of the kings—a pattern which usually includes most or all of the following elements:

- Who the king was, in terms of his relationship to the former king
- Over what kingdom he reigned

- When he became king, in terms of the regnal year of a king in the other kingdom
- How long he reigned
- Whether he did what was good or evil
- Details of his reign, usually related in terms of the spiritual judgment previously mentioned
- Sources concerning his reign
- Details concerning his death and burial
- His successor.

3. There is a greater emphasis on the work of the prophets in Kings than in Samuel. Here, in connection with the story of the Northern Kingdom, is to be found the stories about Elijah and Elisha. If there are any heroes (besides God) in these books, it is the prophets, not the kings.

OUTLINE

A brief summary of the contents of the two books might be:

- 1 Kings: End of David's reign through the reign of Ahaziah (or perhaps the death of Ahab).
- 2 Kings: Reign of Ahaziah through the beginning of the Babylonian Captivity.

Kings may also be outlined as follows:

- The reign of Solomon (including the transition from David's reign to Solomon's) — 1 Kings 1–11.
- The divided kingdom — 1 Kings 12–2 Kings 17.
- The "Judah Alone" period — 2 Kings 18–25.

PURPOSE

The major purpose of the book seems to be to explain why the kingdoms of God's people were destroyed.

If the prophetic history (Joshua/Judges/Samuel/Kings) can be thought of as the history of the Israelite kingdom which reached its climax during the days of David (see the notes on Samuel), Kings tells the story of the downhill slide of that kingdom into division, destruction, and disgrace. Even the glories of the reign of Solomon can be seen, in retrospect, to be only ephemeral, without a solid foundation.

The Jews of the Exile must have wondered: How could this have happened? We are the people of God, descended from Abraham and Israel, heirs of the glorious kingdom of David and Solomon, and recipients of all the promises made by God to our fathers through all the years. How is it that our kingdom, our temple, and our holy city could have been destroyed and that we, God's chosen ones, could have been carried away into captivity? *Kings was written to answer those questions.*

In doing so, it makes it plain that the destruction of the kingdoms was the result of disobedience to God. Consequently, from a practical standpoint, along with the other former prophets, *it teaches that disobedience brings condemnation and that sin always has negative consequences.* (The writer of Kings also believes that obedience results in blessings, but there are few examples of obedience and blessings in these books.)

Furthermore, *it demonstrates that God is in control of human history*. The first readers might have been wondering if, in fact, their God, Yahweh, might be weaker than the gods of the Babylonians in whose land the Israelites were living, since the customary wisdom of the ANE held that the gods of the nation that won in battle had triumphed over the gods of the defeated nation. If so, Kings would have disabused them of that notion, since it teaches that the destruction of Israel was not accidental, nor did it come about because other nations (and their gods) were stronger than Yahweh. Rather, they would have learned that God is in charge of the world, that He is responsible for what happened to Israel, and that He had used other nations to punish His people.

KINGS AND THE NEW TESTAMENT

Elijah is mentioned in the New Testament (see Jas 5:17), and is compared to Jesus in Matthew 16.

MEMORABLE PASSAGES

1 Kings 18:21; 1 Kings 19:11–12; 2 Kings 5:10–11; 2 Kings 6:16–17; 2 Kings 7:9; 2 Kings 17:7; 2 Kings 22:8, 11.

DISCUSSION QUESTIONS

1. Discuss the end of David's reign and the beginning of Solomon's reign. Why do David's actions seem out of keeping with his character, as previously revealed? How is Solomon pictured in this story?
2. Discuss the reign of Solomon. Was Solomon a "good king" or a "bad king"? Compare Solomon's achievements with Samuel's warning concerning what a king would do and with Deuteronomy 17. In what sense did the glories of Solomon's kingdom rest on a weak foundation?
3. A considerable amount of space is given in Kings to the relationship of Israel's kings to the kings of Syria. Why should the kings of Syria receive so much attention in this history?

4. The major spiritual battle that occurs in Kings is between Yahweh and his prophets and the Baals. Discuss this battle. Who or what were the Baals? What was the danger—what was at stake in the battle? What were the high points and/or low points in this battle? When and how was the final victory won by and for Yahweh?
5. Which of the writing prophets preached during the period of time covered by the books of 1 and 2 Kings? What message did each proclaim?
6. Put yourself in the place of one of the first readers of this book (along with the other books of the former prophets) and think of what you read from—say—the standpoint of a Jew in Babylon in 550 BC. How would you feel? What would you conclude? How might you react? Would there be any comforting thoughts from the work?

NOTES ON THE DIVIDED KINGDOM

Southern Kingdom   Northern Kingdom
   Name: Judah   Israel (also called: Ephraim, after the leading tribe; Samaria, after the capital city.)
   Beginning: ca. 930/920 BC   ca. 930/920 BC
   No. of Tribes: One (or Two)   Ten
   Capital: Jerusalem   Shechem; Tirzah; Samaria

Kings*:
Southern (Judah)	Northern (Israel)
Rehoboam, 922–915	Jeroboam I, 922–901
Abijah, 915–913	Nadab, 901–900
Asa, 913–873	Baasha, 900–877
Jehoshaphat, 873–849	Elah, 877–816
Jehoram, 849–842	Zimri, 876
Ahaziah, 842	Omri, 876–869
Athaliah, 842–837	Ahab, 869–850
Joash, 837–800	Ahaziah, 850–849
Amaziah, 800–783	Jehoram, 849–842
Uzziah (Azariah), 783–742	Jehu, 842–815
(Jotham coregent ca. 750)	Jehoahaz, 815–801

Jotham, 742–735
Ahaz, 735–715
Hezekiah, 715–687/86
Manasseh, 687/86–642
Amon, 642–640
Josiah, 640–609
Jehoahaz, 609
Jehoiakim, 609–598
Jehoiachin, 598/87
Zedekiah, 597–587
Beginning of Exile, 587

Jehoash, 801–786
Jeroboam II, 786–746
Zechariah, 746–745
Shallum, 745
Menahem, 745–738
Pekahiah, 738–737
Pekah, 737–732
Hoshea, 732–724
Fall of Samaria, 721

Dynasties:
   One—all from David   Several ended:
   ca. 587/586 BC   ca. 721 BC (This brought the period of the Divided Kingdom to an end; the following period is called the "Judah Alone" period.)
   Lasted:
   ca. 340 years until Babylonian captivity, but the Jews who returned considered themselves the continuation of this kingdom — ca 200 years
   Conquered, taken captive by:
     Babylonia   Assyria
   Returned from captivity?
     Yes   No

*Dates are from John Bright, *A History of Israel*, Chronological Charts.

THE BOOKS OF 1 AND 2 CHRONICLES
The Temple

NAME

The meaning of the Hebrew title for Chronicles is "Words of the Days." But the Hebrew word used for "word" in this verse—*DABAR*—means something more than "word." It can also mean "happening." So the title in Hebrew means, not just "Words," but "Events of the Days." Thus, the title in Hebrew is very similar to the meaning of the English title, which is derived from the title given to the books by Jerome in the Latin Vulgate. The Septuagint calls Chronicles "Things Passed Over," suggesting that the translators viewed these books as supplemental to Samuel and Kings.

CONTENTS, EMPHASIS

The primary message of Chronicles has to do with the temple.

Several other things are emphasized in the book, but most of them can be seen as having to do with the temple. For instance, the role of the Levites is emphasized, but they served in the temple. The opposition to false gods and adherence to the law of God are also emphasized, but these, too, are closely linked to the true worship of God according to the law of God—which takes place in the temple, the house of God.

The book tells this story: The genealogies bring us to the death of Saul and the inauguration of David's kingdom. Very early we read about David's bringing the ark to Jerusalem, and then of his desire to build the temple. David isn't allowed to build the temple; his son Solomon is to do that. But the last part of 1 Chronicles is altogether about David's preparations for its building, made on behalf of Solomon.

In 2 Chronicles, the story of Solomon's reign to a great extent features the story of his building of the temple. Then the rest of 2 Chronicles is taken up with the story of the kings of Judah who were descended from David and Solomon. Many of them were evil. But the reigns of the evil kings are usually passed over quickly, whereas more time and space is given to the good kings. And special attention is focused on the reigns of Asa, Jehoshaphat, Hezekiah, and Josiah. The good kings are those who kept the law of God, opposed idolatry, and refused to make alliances with other nations. A number of them repaired the temple of the Lord. (2 Chron 15:8; 24:4; 29:3; 34:8)

Then, when we come to the last chapter of the book, within four verses of the end, we find these words: "[The Babylonians] burned the house of God ..." Finally, the book ends with Cyrus' proclamation that "the Lord, the God of heaven, ... has charged me *to build him a house at Jerusalem*, which is in Judah. Whoever is among you of all his people, may the Lord his God be with him. Let him go up." (2 Chron 36:23, emphasis added)

You could say that *Chronicles is a history of the house of God, the temple of Yahweh, from its construction to its destruction, with a preliminary note about its reconstruction.* The story of the temple is at the heart of the message of Chronicles.

CLASSIFICATION

The two books of Chronicles were originally one book in the Hebrew Bible; it was only divided into two books when it was translated into Greek because the size of the book made it necessary to use two scrolls for it. 1 and 2 Chronicles are classified as books of history in the English Old Testament. In the Hebrew Bible, Chronicles is the last book of the Writings (the Kethubim), which is the third of the three divisions of the Hebrew Bible. (Samuel and Kings are part of the "Former Prophets;" Chronicles is not.)

DATE AND AUTHOR

Scholars agree on one point: Chronicles is one of the later books of the Old Testament (some think it may be the latest written); it is certainly a post-exilic work. Beyond that, there are a variety of opinions on this subject, even among conservative scholars. Some accept a fourth-century BC date for the book (Leslie Allen, *1, 2 Chronicles*, The Communicator's Commentary, 10 [Waco, TX: Word Books, 1987]), and another very common view is that Chronicles was written about 400 BC.

Others believe that the author of Chronicles was Ezra. If Ezra was the author, the date of his return to Judah from Babylon (as recorded in the last few chapters of Ezra) occurred about 457 BC. Thus, the book of Chronicles would have been written sometime after that. According to this view, Chronicles was possibly written about 450–425 BC.

The introduction to Chronicles in *Expositors Bible Commentary* speaks of some of the reasons for thinking of Ezra as the author. First, Jewish tradition "affirms that Ezra wrote Chronicles, along with the book that bears his name." [J. Barton Payne, "1, 2 Chronicles," *Expositors Bible Commentary*, 4, (Grand Rapids, MI: Zondervan, 1988), 305–306]. Furthermore, the literary style of the two books is similar; they share similar interests and concerns; and Ezra is obviously intended to be a continuation of Chronicles since the last two verses of Chronicles are the same as the first verses of Ezra (Payne, 305).

However, there are also arguments against Ezra's authorship. For instance, the similarity between the vocabulary of Ezra and Chronicles has been questioned. But one of the most important arguments against Ezra's authorship has to do with the historical situation presupposed by the book. Specifically, the author of Ezra-Nehemiah was very concerned about mixed marriages. If the same person also wrote Chronicles, he had a perfect example of the sinful consequences of such marriages in Solomon. But Chronicles fails to mention this sin of Solomon! (Payne, 306–307) This would argue against the Ezra-Nehemiah historical situation providing the background for the writing of Chronicles.

Furthermore, the fact that Ezra begins as Chronicles ends does not altogether prove that Ezra was the author, especially since Chronicles is placed at the very end of the Hebrew Bible, as the last book of the third division, the writings (Payne, 307). Ezra-Nehemiah, therefore, comes before Chronicles in the Hebrew scriptures! That means that in the Hebrew Bible (unlike the English Old Testament) one would not read directly from Chronicles to Ezra. He would read Ezra-Nehemiah first, and then read Chronicles.

Another view has it that Chronicles was written about 515 BC, about the time that the Jews completed the temple, twenty or so years after their first return from Babylonian captivity. In favor of that view, it should be remembered that Chronicles is primarily about the temple. If Chronicles was written about the time the rebuilding of the temple was completed, then the importance of the temple, so stressed in Chronicles, *would* speak to the Jews' situation: It would remind them, by giving the history of the temple, of their connection with the glorious days when Solomon's temple was still standing.

SOURCES

The writer obviously used canonical books as sources—especially Samuel and Kings, but other books as well, including the Pentateuch. In addition to Samuel/Kings, the author cites a number of sources that apparently were used in the writing. Specifically mentioned are:

- The official records of kings, variously referred to as "The Book of the Kings of Israel and Judah," "The Book of the Kings of Judah and Israel," "The Chronicles of King David," etc.
- Official genealogies, taken, for the most part, from the Pentateuch.
- Prophetic records, including writings attributed to "Samuel, Nathan, Gad, Ahijah, Shemaiah, Iddo, Jehu, and Isaiah."

(*HSB*) See, for example, the last two verses of 1 Chronicles.

RELATIONSHIP TO OTHER HISTORICAL BOOKS

Chronicles, to some extent, repeats the material in Samuel and Kings, and then Ezra takes up the story just where Chronicles leaves off. The closing verses of Chronicles are repeated as the opening verses of Ezra.

Thus, Chronicles forms a unit with Ezra and Nehemiah in a way similar to the way Samuel and Kings are related to Joshua and Judges. The four books Joshua/Judges/Samuel/Kings—the former prophets in the Hebrew Bible—tell the story of Israel from conquest to captivity, concluding about 560 BC.

On the other hand, if the nine chapters of genealogies are ignored, Chronicles/Ezra/Nehemiah begins later than Samuel-Kings, since it starts with the death of Saul which is found at the very end of 1 Samuel, and then continues beyond the story of Samuel and Kings to the history of the several returns from Babylonian captivity and the period of the restoration, concluding with Nehemiah's reforms about 445 BC or later.

So the Old Testament provides, in a sense, two overlapping histories: On one hand, the former prophets, recording Hebrew history from conquest to captivity and concluding about 560 BC; and, on the other hand, the unit of Chronicles/Ezra/Nehemiah, recording the same history from the beginning of David's kingdom to the restoration in Judah, perhaps about 445 BC.

While Chronicles retells part of the story told in Samuel and Kings, it differs from Samuel and Kings in several ways. Chronicles:

- Emphasizes the genealogies, the temple, the Davidic line, the Levites, and, in general, priestly concerns.
- Begins at a different point; it says almost nothing about Saul.
- Almost completely ignores the Northern Kingdom of Israel.
- Doesn't mention the blatant sins of David and Solomon.
- Differs from Samuel/Kings, according to *HSB*, in that its "numbers are in round figures and generally larger."

Furthermore, although it omits some things found in Samuel/Kings, it also includes some information not found in the other books. For example, it is only in Chronicles that one can learn that David was not allowed to build the temple because he was a man of blood, or violence, and God wanted a man of peace—namely Solomon—to build His temple. (See 1 Chron 22:8.) Likewise, many other facts are revealed in Chronicles that are not found in Samuel or Kings.

In addition, through the genealogies at the beginning of 1 Chronicles, it covers a broader scope of history than Samuel/Kings. In fact, the books of Chronicles, Ezra, and Nehemiah form a unit that tells the story of the history of the Jews from the beginning of the world to the end of the Old Testament era. In a sense, Chronicles covers the same ground (and then some) and provides an alternative history to the Primary History, found in Genesis through 2 Kings.

OUTLINE

It is possible to say that 1 Chronicles is about David's kingdom through David's death and that 2 Chronicles covers the period of time from Solomon's kingdom through the Babylonian captivity. The following four-point outline is worth remembering:

- The genealogies — 1 Chronicles 1–9.
- The reign of David — 1 Chronicles 10–29.
- The reign of Solomon — 2 Chronicles 1–9.
- The kingdom of Judah — 2 Chronicles 10–36.

PURPOSES

Various purposes for the book have been proposed by different authors.

1. Some see its purpose as being primarily *historical* and *supplementary*: to complete the historical record of the Jewish people. It was written to "fill in the blanks" left in the history written to that time. (See *Halley's Bible Handbook*.)

2. Others see a *didactic* or *hortatory* purpose in its writing. Of the returned exiles, *EHB* says:

> They needed to know the right lines on which to re-establish patterns of worship. And they needed most of all to be reminded of the greatest lesson their history had to teach: that prosperity and well-being depend absolutely on faithfulness to God. Idolatry and neglect of God's law always has and always will result in judgement and disaster. (*EHB*, 286)

LaSor, in *Old Testament Survey,* suggests that the Chronicler's aim is to teach the people something:

> The Chronicler's overarching concern is the theocratic character of the community. God's direct activity, the pattern of retribution, scriptural authority, and centrality of the temple are all components in the rule of God over his people. The Chronicler longs for and seeks to contribute to a recovery of the glorious days of David and Solomon—not by a reestablishment of the monarchy but by a return to obedient worship. (636–637)

3. Some think they see in Chronicles an *eschatological* purpose. That is, they believe that the writer wanted to prepare the people for the coming of a Davidic king and the restoration of the Davidic kingdom. Ellison seems to embrace this view when he writes that the Chronicler "wrote a history of both [the Davidic dynasty and the temple], so that men might recognise that if the Temple had been restored, then a restoration of the monarchy might be confidently expected." (87; see also LaSor, 636–637.)

4. The view of this author is that the purpose of the Chronicler is *practical*. That purpose must be distinguished from his theme. His theme is "the temple," but by dwelling on the temple

he hoped to do two things for his readers: *He wanted to (a) comfort and encourage and (b) warn the restored Israelites.*

First, he desired *to comfort and encourage* his readers. The restored community was poor and few and, for the most part, dispirited. Though in their homeland, they were a captive people, unable to complete any project without the approval of their Persian overlords. In general, the Chronicler sought to link them with a more glorious past to encourage them in their despondency. Allen, in his commentary, says that the author wrote for the post-exilic community which had become acutely appreciative of the past: "in an insecure period when morale must often have been low, it gave them something firm to cling to." (17)

In particular, Chronicles proclaims that they were attached to the promised line that descended from Adam, through Abraham and Israel. The genealogies reminded them that, of all the descendants of Adam, they were the only chosen people! And their recently constructed temple made it possible for them to share in the glorious history of the original temple, as that story is told in Chronicles. Chronicles had an encouraging message for them! (Cf. Ellison, 86–87.)

But he must also have wanted *to warn* his readers. One temple had been built, but it had been destroyed, because the people would not listen to the voice of God or to the law of God (see 2 Chron 36:15–16). So the Chronicler was saying to the returned Jews, now that the temple has been completed, you cannot be complacent! He may be saying: The same God who destroyed the temple before can destroy it again if you today fail to listen to the voice of God or to obey the law of God.

CHRONICLES AND THE NEW TESTAMENT

The *EBC* says that, according to one source, the New Testament quotes from Chronicles 68 times. It should also be noted that the church in the New Testament is likened to the Old Testament temple.

DISCUSSION QUESTIONS

1. Why does Chronicles begin with nine chapters of genealogies? What purpose do these genealogies serve?
2. Why are there so many differences between Chronicles, on one hand, and Samuel/Kings, on the other?
3. Discuss the question: Can we depend on the historical accuracy of Chronicles?
4. If we admit that the writer of Chronicles used sources in writing the book, do we thereby question the inspiration of Chronicles?
5. Since the Chronicler obviously writes with a theological purpose in mind, should we question his writing as a historical work? Does writing with such a purpose invalidate the possibility of his recounting the facts of history accurately?
6. Is it possible to explain why the Chronicler omits the sins of David and Solomon?
7. Discuss the problem of the large numbers found in the book of Chronicles (usually higher than those found in Samuel/Kings).
8. Discuss the purpose or purposes of Chronicles. What was Chronicles designed to accomplish? What's the basic message of the book?
9. What are practical or spiritual lessons we can learn from the building of and worship in the temple?

THE BOOK OF EZRA
Return to the Land, Rebuilding the Temple

NAME, CLASSIFICATION

The book is named for its main character, Ezra. Ezra was a priest and scribe (7:11) who returned to Jerusalem from Babylon with a contingent of Jews long after the first return, for the purpose of teaching God's law and requiring the Jews to obey it (7:7–26). He (and the "Great Synagogue") is credited with putting much of the Old Testament together into its final canonical form.

Ezra and Nehemiah are classified as "Writings" (Kethubim) in the Hebrew Bible. In the English Bible, they are classified as "History." "Writings" is the miscellaneous classification. Why are the books in that category so classified? One possibility is that these books were not completed or collected until after the prophets were already a completed unit.

RELATIONSHIP TO OTHER BOOKS

Ezra and Nehemiah were originally one book in the Hebrew Bible. Together they form a unit with Chronicles. The last two verses of 2 Chronicles are identical to the first two verses of Ezra.

In the Hebrew Bible, Ezra/Nehemiah come before Chronicles. Why? Perhaps because they cover a historical period that follows after the history recorded in Samuel/Kings.

EMPHASIS

The book of Ezra, in general, could be said to be about *the re-establishment of Israel's religion*. During their time in Babylonian captivity, the Jews had not deserted their God or their religion, but they had been deprived of some of the outward symbols of that religion. With their return, some of those symbols were restored.

Specifically, the book indicates that religion was re-established by

- their return to the promised land,
- their rebuilding of the temple, and
- their repentance.

Underlying the reforms was an emphasis on the law of God (Ezra 7:10). That law undergirded the religious revival of Israel and its keeping became the object of that revival.

AUTHOR, DATE. SOURCES, LANGUAGES

Because of the close relationship between Ezra/Nehemiah and Chronicles—because, e.g., of their similar interests and concerns and of the similarity in their language—, it is often (or usually) assumed that the author of Chronicles also wrote Ezra and Nehemiah. In fact, the author of all three of these books is sometimes thought to be Ezra himself. If Ezra was the author, then all the books must have been written about the same time —perhaps about 450 to 425 BC.

However, some scholars doubt that Ezra is the author of Chronicles and date Chronicles either earlier or later than Ezra. (See the notes on Chronicles.)

If the author of Chronicles is not Ezra, this fact does not affect the question of the authorship of the combined book of Ezra/Nehemiah. It should be noted that numerous documents are used in these two books—including the memoirs of Ezra (see the chapters in Ezra and Nehemiah in which Ezra speaks in the first person), the memoirs of Nehemiah (see the chapters in which Nehemiah speaks in the first person), lists, and official letters and documents (see, e.g., Ezra 7:11–26). Thus, the writer —whether he was Ezra or someone else—was both an author and a compiler.

Ezra is unusual in that portions of the book are written in Aramaic; almost all of the rest of the Old Testament was written in Hebrew.

HISTORICAL SETTING

God caused the kingdom of Judah to be destroyed and its people to be taken captive by the Babylonians, because of the sins of His people. The final destruction of Jerusalem and the temple and the deportation of the people occurred about 587 or 586 BC.

The Jews were in captivity for several decades. Although it was a difficult time for them, during the exile significant positive changes occurred which were to have a major impact on their religion from that time on.

While the Jews were in Babylon, a coalition of Medes and Persians overcame the Babylonians and took over their kingdom. Eventually, this became the Persian Empire, the greatest empire in existence to that time.

Cyrus (who was unknowingly doing Yahweh's bidding) allowed the Jews to return to their homeland in about 538 BC. This was in keeping with Persian policy, just as their deportation had been in keeping with Babylonian policy. This, the first return of the Jews, is described in Ezra 1–2.

When they returned, the Jews were few, poor, and weak. They were still under their Persian overlords. Furthermore, they were opposed by the people who were already living in the land, descendants of those whom the Assyrians had settled there, and the Jews and Israelites who had remained in the land after the Northern and Southern Kingdoms had been deported.

Nevertheless, the Jews embarked on their first major project: rebuilding the temple. The foundation of the temple was laid (Ezra 3), but opposition from others in the land proved effective, and the work of rebuilding halted for the next fifteen or sixteen years (Ezra 4).

About 520 BC there arose the prophets Haggai and Zechariah to encourage the completion of the temple. With their urging, work was begun again and the temple was finally completed and dedicated about 516 BC. (Ezra 5–6)

Almost sixty years later Ezra was commissioned by the Persian ruler to return to Jerusalem, to make sacrifices, and to teach and enforce the Law. (Ezra 7) He returned about 457 BC, and several hundred other Jews accompanied him.

Upon his arrival in the land, Ezra discovered that the Jews had not kept the law. Consequently, he instituted reforms, especially involving the dissolution of mixed marriages.

OUTLINE

The book is divided into two parts, and each part has a different emphasis.

- Part One tells of the return in 538 BC — Ezra 1–6.

- Part Two tells of Ezra's return about 457 BC and of the reforms he instituted — Ezra 7–10.

PURPOSE

The purpose of the book is *to describe how Israel, without monarchy or independence, although small and poor and almost helpless, survived as the people of God by becoming a religious community centered around a law, rather than a nation centered around a king and territory.*

DISCUSSION QUESTIONS

1. What is the language "Aramaic"? How is it related to Hebrew? What passages in Ezra are written in Aramaic? What portions of the rest of the Old Testament are written in Aramaic? How can the Aramaic portions of Ezra be explained? Why are those particular portions in Aramaic?
2. What positive results came about because of the years the Jews spent in Babylonian exile?
3. Some question whether Ezra should come before Nehemiah or after. What are the arguments for saying that Ezra should be after Nehemiah rather than before it? How can those arguments be answered?
4. To many, the dissolution of the mixed marriages in Ezra and Nehemiah causes problems: Isn't this a rather drastic action? What about the children who were born into these marriages? Does this reflect a prejudicial attitude towards the Gentiles, simply because they were Gentiles?
5. How does Ezra lead the Jews into a period of repentance and reform?

6. Compare and contrast Ezra's work and reforms with Nehemiah's work and reforms.
7. What is the history of the temple? What temple was rebuilt in the book of Ezra? When had it been destroyed? How does the temple relate to the tabernacle and the synagogue? What happened to the temple that was rebuilt when the Jews returned?

THE BOOK OF NEHEMIAH
Rebuilding the Walls, Renewing the Covenant

NAME, CLASSIFICATION

The book is named after Nehemiah, its main character, whose name means "whom God has comforted." In the English Old Testament, it is classified as one of the books of history; in the Hebrew Bible, it is found among the Writings. The Hebrew Bible includes Nehemiah as a part of the book of Ezra, and the two books are closely related to Chronicles. The situation pictured in Nehemiah also has much in common with the sins of Judah which are described in the book of Malachi.

CONTENTS, EMPHASIS

Nehemiah is about two things: chapters. 1–7: Rebuilding the walls of Jerusalem, in the 20th year of Artaxerxes (1:1; 2:1), at the third return, ca. 445 BC. Chapters 8–13: Renewal of the covenant, including religious reforms.

The emphasis may be said to be *the renewal of the covenant relationship with God*. Just as the rebuilding of the temple in Ezra facilitated the religious revival that the book tells about, so the rebuilding of the walls in Nehemiah facilitates the renewal of the covenant by providing a safe place where the Jews will be free from outside interference to keep the terms of the covenant made between God and Israel long before (Exod 19).

AUTHOR AND DATE

Since Nehemiah was originally part of a work that included Ezra, the two-part work was written/compiled by the same author. Its close connection with Chronicles has led many to think that all three books were written by the same person. And Ezra has been thought to be the "Chronicler" responsible for Chronicles/Ezra/Nehemiah. For a consideration of these views, see the notes on Chronicles and Ezra.

Concerning the author and date of Ezra/Nehemiah, three things seem certain: (1) he used a number of sources, including the memoirs of both Ezra and Nehemiah. (2) He wrote very late in Judah's history; some have dated the work to about 400 BC. (3) He was interested in or concerned about several things:

- God's overruling care of the Jews was manifested in the Persian kings' favorable decisions regarding the Jews.
- The law of God.
- Worship, the temple, the Levites, the priesthood.
- Abstaining from contaminating associations with other peoples.
- Jerusalem.
- The Sabbath.
- The covenant.

HISTORICAL SETTING

The first return occurred about 538 BC and was led by Sheshbazzar and Zerubbabel. The major task of the Jews at that time was rebuilding the temple. This was completed about 516 BC.

But the Jews after their return were still a captive people under the control of the Persian empire. They were poor, few, and dispirited. More importantly, the book of Nehemiah presents them as defenseless, especially in that, with the walls of Jerusalem broken down, the city was easy prey for any army or gang of marauders.

The second return mentioned is Ezra's return, about 457 BC. Ezra's purpose was to teach and enforce the law. As a part of that task, he instituted reforms. However, the Jews apparently did not remain faithful to their religion or continue to follow Ezra's instructions.

Nehemiah was cupbearer to the king of Persia (1:11), a position of importance and honor, living in Susa, the capital of the Empire. Hearing of the sad state of the Jews, he asked to go and help them. At his request, the king allowed him to return to Jerusalem in about 445 BC for the purpose of rebuilding its walls. There he became, by the authority of the king of the Persian empire, the governor of the land (10:1).

The book of Nehemiah tells how he accomplished two tasks: the rebuilding of the walls of Jerusalem and the renewal of the covenant.

About 432 BC Nehemiah went back to the Persian king, only to discover on his return to Judah that the Jews had apostatized (13:6–7). The book ends with a record of the reforms he carried out at that time.

It is interesting that in a number of ways (e.g., concern for the Sabbath, for tithing, and for remaining separate from foreigners) Nehemiah anticipates the interests and concerns of the Jews during the days of Jesus.

EXPANDED OUTLINE

A. Rebuilding the walls.

- Nehemiah's return — chapters 1:1–2:10. This is the third return mentioned in the Bible.
- Rebuilding completed in spite of opposition — chapters 2:11–7:73.

B. Renewal of the covenant.
1. Preparation for renewing the covenant:

- Reading of the law — chapter 8:1–12.
- Keeping Feast of Tabernacles — chapter 8:13–18.

2. Making the covenant:

- Preparation: Cleansing the community of foreigners — chapter 9:1–5.
- The covenant proposed: historical prologue — chapter 9:6–38.
- The covenant accepted: by the leaders (chapter 10:1–27) and then by all the people — chapter 10:28–29.
- d. Specific provisions of the covenant:

1. Remain separate from foreigners — chapter 10:30.
2. Not profane the Sabbath — chapter 10:31.
3. Meet financial obligations—to priesthood and temple — chapter 10:32–39.

e. Provisions to assure the observance of the covenant.

- Repopulating Jerusalem — chapter 11:1–36.
- Dedicating the walls — chapter 12:1–47.

3. Breaking of the covenant. Nehemiah went back to Artaxerxes (chapter 13:6-7); while he was gone, the Jews apostatized and failed to keep their promises.

4. Enforcing the covenant: reforms initiated — chapter 13:1-31.

- Preliminary statement — chapter 13:1-3.
- Casting Tobiah out of the temple — chapter 13:4-9.
- Assuring the priests' support — chapter 13:10-14.
- Making sure the Sabbath is kept — chapter 13:15-22.
- Breaking up marriages with foreign women — chapter 13:23-31.

PURPOSE

The purpose of the book is *to demonstrate that Israel is still the people of God, through the covenant relationship that had been instituted on Mt. Sinai which is here renewed.* The Jews who read these words would have been comforted (note Nehemiah's name) by being reminded of that covenant and Israel's participation in it.

There is, however, in the final chapter of the history of Israel written in the Old Testament (Nehemiah 13) also another solemn reminder: *Israel never kept the covenant perfectly.* Anyone reading these words should have been caused (by a consideration of that fact) to look for a better system for remaining on good terms with God.

DISCUSSION QUESTIONS

1. Why was Jerusalem in dire danger because its walls were broken down? How were the walls rebuilt? What lessons can we learn from this example, especially regarding leadership?

2. What kind of sins were found in the reform community, as contrasted with the sins of the pre-exilic community?
3. How can Nehemiah be connected with the prophet Malachi?
4. How are the Jews in this book like the Jews of the New Testament?
5. Why were the foreign wives put away? (13:26) Was this largely a matter of racial prejudice? Was it a mistaken policy? Were these wives who had converted to Judaism or were they still pagans?
6. When the Old Testament says that the Jews made a covenant with God, what does it mean? Does it mean that this is a new covenant? Or is this another way of saying that they simply agreed to the terms of an earlier covenant? What were the terms of the Mosaic covenant, according to Exodus 19?

THE BOOK OF ESTHER

How God Saved the Jews from Destruction

NAME, CLASSIFICATION

The book is named after its main character, Esther, whose name is a Persian word meaning "star." Her Hebrew name "Hadassah" means "Myrtle." In the Hebrew Bible, Esther is classified among the "Writings." It is one of the "Megilloth," the scrolls, the five little books, each of which was read on a special feast day of the Jews. Esther is read at the Feast of Purim. In the English Old Testament, Esther is classified among the books of history.

EMPHASIS

The major emphasis of the book is the salvation of the Jews from annihilation, accomplished by God through Esther. All that precedes the Jews' deliverance—Esther's becoming queen, the hostility of Haman towards Mordecai and towards the Jews, the appeal to Esther to go to the king, etc.—sets the stage for it.

Perhaps the most interesting thing about the book is that the name of God is not found in it. Still, God is in the book. His hand is seen moving through it (see, e.g., Esth 4:13-14)—and the first readers would have discerned that He was at work in the events it narrates to produce the final result.

AUTHOR, DATE, STYLE

The author is unknown. Probably the book was written close to the time of the events that it records. Those events are thought to have occurred about 480 BC. Scholars say that the literary style in the Hebrew language is outstanding.

HISTORICAL SETTING

The Persians, after taking over the Babylonian Empire, extended their rule over other nations until the Persian Empire was greater than any that had existed to that time. They expanded westward as far as Greece, with which they fought a series of wars before withdrawing further eastward into what is today part of Turkey.

The Jews, throughout the post-exilic period, were subject to the Persians. Cyrus allowed the Jews to return home in about 538 BC. It is evident from the narrative of the first return (Ezra 1–2) that not all of the Jews chose to move back to Judah. Two other returns are mentioned in the Bible: Ezra returned about 457 BC and Nehemiah about 445 BC.

Even though some of the Jews were living again in Palestine, it is clear that there were other Jews scattered throughout the Empire. For instance, in the fourth century BC there was a Jewish colony with a temple at Elephantine in Egypt.

The book of Esther is set in Susa, the capital city of the Persian Empire, during the reign of Ahasuerus, who is usually known as Xerxes, perhaps about 480 BC, after the first return of the Jews, but before Ezra and Nehemiah returned to Palestine.

The book tells how a Jewish maiden named Esther became queen and saved the Jews from an attempt to destroy them.

OUTLINE

The book is a narrative that takes the form of a short novel, the plot of which furnishes an outline for the book.

The first two chapters (which by themselves tell an interesting story) set the stage for the action of the novel. Chapter 3 contains the "precipitating incident"—the event or incident that provides the problem or complication which in turn motivates or leads to all else that occurs in the story. Then chapters 4–10 show how the problem that arises from the precipitating incident is solved, with the result that the "good guys" are saved—and, in fact, are better off than they were before. So the outline is:

- Esther becomes queen — chapters 1–2.
- Haman plots to destroy the Jews — chapter 3.
- The Jews are saved by Esther — chapters 4–10.

PURPOSE

The main purpose of the book may have been to assure the readers that, in spite of their scattering, God was still watching over them and could and would still deliver them, even in unpromising circumstances, by using unexpected means or methods.

The book serves other purposes as well.

From a historical standpoint, it explains the origin of the Feast of Purim. This feast did not originate in the Law given by God to Israel through Moses in the Pentateuch. Yet it was observed in later years. How did it originate? Esther answers that question. The book of Esther also tells something about the history of the Jews during the post-exilic period.

From a literary standpoint, it is interesting, even entertaining. Literary techniques abound in the work. Among them are:

- Suspense — Will Esther agree to go into the king even though it may mean her life? If she goes, will the king agree to save the Jews?
- Irony — Haman is hanged on the gallows he built for Mordecai.
- Humor (achieved through irony) — Haman has to lead Mordecai—the person he hates more than anyone else in the world—through the city, with Mordecai seated on the king's horse and Haman shouting his praises.
- Foreshadowing — Mordecai saves the king's life, and the fact is written down early in the book, but only becomes important later in the plot.
- Well-drawn characters — When we read about Mordecai and Haman, the kind of people they are sticks with us and we remember them.
- "Cinderella" plot — The poor little orphan girl becomes queen of the mighty Persian Empire.
- Vice is punished, virtue rewarded — Haman's jealousy leads to his downfall; Mordecai and Esther are the "good guys," and they win in the end.

What's the value of being interesting, even entertaining? The book has truth to teach. To make that truth interesting or entertaining is to make it more likely to be learned and remembered.

How should those who accept the Bible as inspired by God feel about the obvious literary artistry of Esther (and of other Old Testament books or parts of books)? If we say that something is artistically written and uses literary devices, do we thereby question its authenticity? Not necessarily.

After all, in the New Testament we have great literature (see, e.g., 1 Cor 13) as well as great religious teachings. The parables are effectively told stories, using literary artistry. In general, then, we can say that God's inspiration does not preclude the possibility that what an inspired person writes will also be great literature.

Likewise in the Old Testament, the facts concerning Esther were plain. But how those facts were put together—with or without suspense, irony, humor, etc.—depends on the author (just as, given the same facts, some people can make a good story out of an event—without lying or stretching the truth—, but others can't). God could use a gifted author to create an inspired work of great literature.

From a theological standpoint, the book demonstrates:

1. How the Jews escaped annihilation on one occasion. This was significant in that their deliverance kept the hope of the promises of God alive. It was from such hope that expectations of a coming Messiah arose.
2. How God can work providentially to accomplish His will, even in an alien environment.
3. How the Gentiles are related to God and to the Jews: (a) Some of the Gentiles are enemies of the Jews. God achieves His purposes in spite of them, and, in fact, they are killed. (b) Some of them are friends of the Jews. God in their case uses them to achieve His purposes—e.g., the man who was in charge of the Persian king's harem.
4. Some of them become Jews, according to Esther 8:17.

MEMORABLE VERSES

Esther 4:13–14.

DISCUSSION QUESTIONS

1. Liberal scholars have questioned the historicity of Esther. Some have seen the book as a work of fiction intending, perhaps, to teach a lesson. Evaluate the reasons given for these positions.
2. Why would the author have not included the name of God in the book?
3. Discuss the providence of God as it relates to the story told in the book of Esther.
4. Discuss Esther as a work of literature. Can you illustrate more adequately the literary devices mentioned above? Can you find others in the book that ought to be mentioned?
5. How did the Feast of Purim fit into the calendar of feasts in Judaism?
6. Why would Mordecai not bow down to Haman? What does this reflect about Jewish behavior in the period when the book was written?
7. Are we supposed to learn a moral lesson from Vashti's behavior? In what sense is Esther a good example?

INTRODUCTION TO OLD TESTAMENT POETRY

POETRY AS LITERATURE

- Poetry is universal. All societies have and have had poetry.
- Poetry is the oldest form of literature (as contrasted, say, with day-to-day record-keeping).
- Poetry is hard to define, but in general has certain characteristics.

POETRY IN THE OLD TESTAMENT

A. There are five books that are designated "Books of Poetry" in the English Bible.
   1. They are:

   - *Job* — a book about why the righteous suffer.
   - *Psalms* — a book of songs designed to be used in praise to God.

- *Proverbs* — a book of wise sayings intended to teach how to be successful.
- *Ecclesiastes* — a book that deals with the meaning of life.
- *Song of Solomon* — a book of love songs, celebrating romantic love.

2. There are certain inconsistencies in this designation.

- That the Massoretes agreed that Job, Psalms, and Proverbs were poetry is evident from the fact that they printed the text differently to show that these books made up a different genre of literature.
- The book of Ecclesiastes is, for the most part, not regarded as poetry.
- Song of Solomon is usually thought of as great poetry, but it was not put in the same category as Job, Pslams, and Proverbs by the Massoretes.

B. In addition, poetry is found throughout the rest of the Old Testament—in the Pentateuch, in the historical books, and especially in the books of prophecy.

CHARACTERISTICS OF OLD TESTAMENT POETRY

A. We should expect Old Testament poetry to be, in many respects, like all poetry—e.g., in its use of figures of speech.

B. There are also forms that are especially characteristic of Old Testament poetry.

1. Hebrew poetry does not rhyme. It may have rhythm. But its rhythm is chiefly related to the flow of ideas, rather than to a regular metrical system. This flow of ideas is called *parallelism*. Parallelism is the main formal characteristic of Old Testament poetry.

a. The most basic form of parallelism involves two lines of poetry, the second of which has a special relationship to the first. It may repeat the idea found in the first, contrast with the idea found in the first, or complete the idea found in the first.

b. A number of different kinds of parallelism have been identified. Many variations are possible, but the most common types of parallelism are:

- Synonymous — the second line says the same thing as or something very similar to the first line. Psalms 24:1
- Antithetical — the second line contrasts with the first line. Psalms 1:6; Psalms 34:10
- Synthetic — the second line completes the thought of the first line or in some way supplements the first line. Psalms 2:6; Psalms 14:1a
- Climactic, or Stair-like — the second line (and succeeding lines) includes some of the same words as the first line but adds further information to or completes the idea of the first line. Psalms 29:1; Psalms 29:8; Psalms 92:9
- Emblematic — the first line begins with "like" or "as" and the second line completes a comparison begun in the first line. Psalms 42:1; Psalms 103:13
- Inverted — the first part of the first line is parallel to the second part of the second line, and the second part of the first line is parallel to the first part of the second line, in an ABBA pattern. Psalms 51:1; Psalms 91:14

2. Other formal characteristics found in Hebrew poetry include the use of acrostics—in which the lines of a poem begin with the letters of the Hebrew alphabet in order. (The first line begins with the first letter of the Hebrew alphabet, the second line with the second letter, etc.)

3. Some of these forms are also to be found among other peoples of the ANE. The difference between the poetry of other peoples and that of Israel is not so much the form as the content of the poems.

INTERPRETATION OF OLD TESTAMENT POETRY

- It is most important to remember that poetry is not prose, nor should it be interpreted as if it were prose. (See "Book of Psalms.")
- In addition, understanding the forms in which this poetry is written will sometimes help in understanding individual words and phrases.

THE BOOK OF JOB

NAME

The book is named after its central character, Job, whose name "some have taken to mean 'he who turns to God.'" (*HSB*)

CLASSIFICATION

It is classified in the English Bible among the books of poetry, and in the Hebrew Bible among the writings. It is also classified as "wisdom literature."

SETTING

Note that we may believe that there is a difference between the setting of the story and the time of its writing, without rejecting its authenticity or inspiration.

- Where? The story is set in Uz, a land in the East, probably in southeastern Edom.

- When? Apparently in the days before the giving of the Law of Moses, perhaps about the time of Abraham. Why is this conclusion probable?

1. The main characters are not identified as Hebrews, Israelites, or Jews.
2. The story is not set in Palestine or Israel but in the East.
3. No distinction is made between Israelites and non-Israelites.
4. Job (like Abraham and the other patriarchs) offers sacrifices; there apparently is no priestly class for this purpose.
5. Job appears to be the same kind of person as Abraham, living the same kind of life, with herds and flocks like Abraham's.

TIME OF WRITING AND AUTHOR

- Author: "The author of the book is unknown, although Jewish tradition suggested writers from Moses to the time of Ahasuerus." (*HSB*)
- Time of writing: The time of writing is unknown. Job has been thought to be one of the earliest writings of the Hebrew Bible, but *HSB* says, "It was probably written during the Solomonic age."

TYPE OF WRITING

Did this incident really happen? Or is it a kind of parable? An epic to teach a lesson?

    A. Some problems with accepting the book as historical:

- It is unusual to be privileged to see into the courts of heaven and overhear God's dealings with the angelic beings. Where did the writer get this information? (Answer: Obviously the story could have come to men originally only by a direct revelation from God.)
- The dialogue between Job and his three friends does not sound like the way people usually talk. (Answers: [1] These are not common people, but wise men. [2] The dialogue has been written in poetry; undoubtedly it gives the substance of the conversations, though probably in a different form. This is not to say that it misrepresents the facts.)
- Were the people of the ancient Near East capable of reasoning like this, of writing this kind of wisdom literature? (Answer: Literature like this was also being written in other countries—namely, Egypt and Babylonia—about 2,000 BC.)

B. Our best approach is simply to accept it as historical, as did the New Testament writers (see Jas 5:11).

CONTENTS

A. Theme. The book concerns the problem: Why do the righteous suffer? It makes it clear that Job is righteous (Job 1:1, 8; 2:3), but Job suffers greatly. The major part of the book is taken up with a discussion of "why."

- The primary argument of the three friends is that all suffering is the result of sin.
- We might give a variety of other answers to the question "Why do the righteous (or the innocent) suffer?"

- But the book of Job answers the question differently. It teaches:

- *There is no answer to the problem of innocent suffering,* except that God wills it, God knows what He is doing, and it is not appropriate for man to question God's right to do whatever He chooses.
- Man's responsibility when he suffers is to remain faithful.

OUTLINE

Prologue: Job 1–2.

Argument (Discussion, Dialogues): Job 3:1–42:6

A. Three cycles of speeches between Job and his three friends:

1. 1st cycle:

- Job — chapter 3.
- Eliphaz — chapters 4–5.
- Job — chapters 6–7.
- Bildad — chapter 8.
- Job — chapters 9–10.
- Zophar — chapter 11.
- Job — chapters 12–14.

2. 2nd cycle:

- Eliphaz — chapter 15.
- Job — chapters 16–17.
- Bildad — chapter 18.
- Job — chapter 19.
- Zophar — chapter 20.
- Job — chapter 21.

3. 3rd cycle:

- Eliphaz — chapter 22.
- Job — chapters 23–24.
- Bildad — chapter 25.
- Job — chapters 26–31.

B. Elihu's speech —chapters 32–37.
C. God's dialogue with Job — chapters 38:1–42:6.

- God's first reply to Job — chapters 38:1–40:2.
- Job's response — chapter 40:3–5.
- God's second reply to Job — chapters 40:6–41:34.
- Job's second response — chapter 42:1–6.

Epilogue — chapter 42:7–17.

THE BOOK OF PSALMS

THE VALUE OF THE PSALMS

- This is beautiful poetry.
- It has universal appeal because the poet expresses the same kind of emotions we feel—and that all people of every age have felt.
- The book of Psalms is often quoted in the New Testament.

CLASSIFICATION

- Psalms is classified under Poetry in the English Old Testament.
- It is classified among the Writings in the Hebrew Bible. Jesus recognized the Psalms as the main book of that third division of His Bible in Luke 24:44.

INTENDED USE

- In Hebrew the name of the book means "The Book of Praises."
- This was the Jews' songbook. There are, for instance, musical notations to indicate how the individual psalms were to be sung or played.
- Some of these poems also teach (see, e.g. Ps 15), but this does not rule out their being used in worship.
- They were also sung by New Testament Christians. Ephesians 5; Colossians 3.
- We need to remember this original use as we interpret the psalms.

MAIN EMPHASES

- Its main emphasis would be: the adoration and praise of God.
- Another important emphasis is: Humanity's feelings about God. A whole gamut of feelings is expressed: adoration, love, confidence, faith, hope—but also despair, longing, puzzlement, complaint.
- An important theme is found in Psalm 1: "Blessed is the man ... "

STRUCTURE

- The book is divided into five books: Psalms 1–41, 42–72, 73–89, 90–106, 107–150. It is a collection of collections. Each ends with a doxology (a word of glory), and the entire book ends with a doxology (Ps 150).

- Think of a large songbook made up of a combination of several smaller songbooks.

AUTHOR AND TIME OF WRITING

- David is usually thought of as the author of the Psalms. 73 of the Psalms bear his name (though he may not have written all of these). David is elsewhere credited with being a poet and a musician (see 2 Sam 23:1; 1 Sam 16:17–23, et al.). Thus, he was probably the principal (but not the only) author. He may also have been a compiler of Psalms.
- Others are also listed in the headings of the psalms: the sons of Korah, Asaph, Jeduthun, Moses, Heman, Ethan.
- The psalms were written at various times in Israel's history. The age of David was probably the "golden age" of psalm-writing. But some may have been written before. Others were undoubtedly written later; Psalm 137, e.g., dates to the time of the exile.
- Thus, the book of Psalms is best thought of as a compilation of some of the best songs and poetry of Israel written by a variety of authors at different times in Israel's history.

HEADINGS OF THE PSALMS

A. Many of the psalms have headings.

B. These are very ancient but were not part of the original poems.

C. There are various types of headings:

- Historical allusions—3, 7, 18, 34, 51.

- Names of Biblical persons—David, 3–9 (the preposition "of" may not signify authorship).
- Type of Psalm—3–6, 7, etc.
- Headings denoting the right method of rendering a psalm—4, 6, 54–55. These are probably analogous to some of the musical notations in our songbooks. "Selah" is probably a musical notation.

TYPES OF PSALMS

There have been many attempts to classify the Psalms into various categories.

A. Willis, *Insights*:

- Hymns—103, 8.
- Psalms proclaiming God as King—5, 10, 24, 29.
- National Psalms of thanksgiving—66, 124.
- Individual Psalms of thanksgiving—30, 116, 71, 41.
- National laments—44, 60, 74.
- Individual laments—3, 4, 5, 13.
- Penitential Psalms—17, 18, 26.
- Royal Psalms—2, 18, 45, 101.

B. *EHB*:

- Hymns—8, 19, 29.
- Community laments—44, 74.
- Royal Psalms—2, 18, 20, 45.
- Individual laments—3, 7, 13, 25, 51.
- Individual thanksgivings—30, 32, 34.

C. *HSB*:

- Personal Psalms.
- Penitential Psalms.
- Psalms of praise.
- Prayer Psalms.
- Messianic Psalms.
- Historical Psalms.
- Liturgical Psalms.
- Psalms that attribute majesty and power to God.

EXAMPLES OF PSALMS

- 1: The introductory psalm, a theme psalm, a wisdom psalm, because it dwells on an important theme of the wisdom literature.
- 2: A royal psalm (see 2, 6, 7-9), also a Messianic psalm —see Hebrews 1:5.
- 7: An individual lament.
- 8: A hymn.
- 15: Morality in the Psalms, a wisdom psalm.
- 19: A psalm of praise, concerning the works and word of God.
- 22: An individual lament, also a Messianic psalm. (See *EHB*.)
- 23: A psalm of praise, a psalm of faith, the shepherd psalm, the most-loved psalm.
- 24: A psalm proclaiming God as king.
- 32: A penitential psalm.
- 44: A national lament.
- 51: A penitential psalm.
- 72: A royal psalm, a prayer for the king.
- 73: A wisdom psalm, asking the question: Why do the wicked prosper?

- 78: A historical psalm, in which history is used to teach a lesson.
- 83: An imprecatory psalm, in which the psalmist asks God to curse or destroy others.
- 117: The shortest psalm.
- 119: An acrostic psalm. "A Hebrew acrostic is a poem in which each succeeding line, verse, or series of verses begins with the next succeeding letter in the alphabet." (Willis, *Insights*, 10) The longest psalm, a psalm especially praising the word of God.
- 136: A historical psalm, probably sung antiphonally.
- 37: A historical psalm, lamenting the destruction of Jerusalem.
- 150: A psalm of praise, doxology for the entire book.

SUGGESTIONS FOR INTERPRETING THE PSALMS

(See Willis, *Insights*, chapters 1–5, pp. 1–40.)

A. Remember that the Psalms are poetry; they should be interpreted as such. *EHB* quotes C. S. Lewis:

> The psalms are poems, and poems intended to be sung; not doctrinal treatises, not even sermons ... They must be read as poems if they are to be understood ... Otherwise we shall miss what is in them and think we see what is not. (327–328)

B. Identify the setting.
C. Determine the type of psalm.
D. Investigate the structure of the psalm.
E. Determine the meaning of the smaller units: of each couplet or each line, of each sentence, of each word. Ask what the psalm reveals about the author's feelings and intentions.
F. Finally ask: How is the psalm of value to me?

1. Is there a reference to Christ in the psalm? Only the New Testament can say for sure.
2. What does the psalm teach about God and about the relationship between God and the individual and the world?
3. How does the psalm make you feel? Can you derive comfort from it? Does it provide you with a way of expressing your thanksgiving to God?

NOTES ON WISDOM LITERATURE

WRITINGS IN THIS CATEGORY

A. Books classified as "wisdom literature":

1. Three books are always placed in this category: Job, Proverbs, Ecclesiastes.

2. Certain psalms are also thought of as "wisdom psalms." One writer includes Psalms 1, 32, 34, 37, 49, 73, 112, 127–28, and 133 in this grouping. (LaSor, 545) According to LaSor, Psalms are put in this category if they:

- Use "the literary techniques of wisdom."
- Intend to "teach by direct instruction."
- Deal with "themes characteristic of wisdom literature."

3. Song of Solomon is also sometimes included in this category.

4. Two of the apocryphal books are classified as "wisdom literature"—Ecclesiasticus (or Sirach) and Wisdom of Solomon (or The Book of Wisdom).

B. These writings have sometimes been divided into two types:

- "Optimistic"—which seems to say that the righteous always prosper—, and "Pessimistic"—which doubts that viewpoint.
- LaSor speaks of these two types as "proverbial wisdom" and "speculative wisdom." (533–534)

C. They are also called "sapiential books." "Sapient" is defined as "possessing or expressing great sagacity or discernment" and is a synonym for "wise."

THE VALUE OF WISDOM

A. "Wisdom"—which is connected with age, experience, and observation—may not be highly valued in modern Western society—not as highly valued, say, as youth, initiative, drive, energy, and education.

B. But in other societies and ages, including the Old Testament era, it was highly valued.

THE WORD FOR WISDOM

The word was *Hokmah*. In some form (as noun, adjective, or verb), it appears 312 times in the Old Testament. More than half of those occurrences are in Job, Proverbs, and Ecclesiastes. (Crenshaw, 245) There are a number of words which serve as synonyms.

CHARACTERISTICS OF WISDOM

See especially 1 Kings 4:29–34.

A. *Wisdom came from God.* Solomon was the epitome of

wisdom, and his wisdom came from God. 1 Kings 3:3–14. Wisdom was sometimes attributed to God alone. Job 12:13ff; Isaiah 31:2. See also Proverbs 1:7; 2:6; 9:10.

B. *Other peoples had wise men and wrote wisdom literature.* See also 1 Kings 5:7; 10:1–9; 23–25; Job 2.

C. *What one knew about "secular subjects" was a part of wisdom.* This, too, was from God. See 1 Kings 4:32–33.

D. *Wisdom then, as now, resulted from experience and observation and a knowledge of human nature and thus involved the ability to know probable outcomes.* See the case of the baby (1 Kgs 3:16–28. Thus "wise" was thought to be almost synonymous with "old." Or the wise man was at his best in his old age: Job 12:12; 15:10; contrast Job 32:9; Ecclesiastes 4:13.

E. *Wisdom was essentially practical—the skill or ability required to be successful.*

1. Suggestions from various authors:

a. Harrison: "The art of being successful."

b. *ISBE*: "the art of reaching one's end by the use of the right means."

c. Archer:

- Practical precepts based upon canny observation.
- Knowing how to do things well that others could do indifferently if at all.
- The art of getting along successfully with God.
- Applied to people who were able to come up with the right answer in critical situations. Genesis 41:39; 2 Samuel 14:2ff.

2. Some examples of the practical meaning of the word:

- It was applied to those having technical skills. Exodus 31:2ff; Isaiah 40:20. See also: Exodus 35:25ff; 28:3; 1

Kings 7:13-14; Ezekiel 27:8-9; Jerermiah 9:17; 10:9; Proverbs 30:24-28.
- To those who advised kings. Job 39:26; Psalms 136:5. See also 2 Samuel 15:31-17:23; 1 Chronicles 27:32.
- To those with military ability. Isaiah 10:13.
- Of lower animals' intelligence. Proverbs 30:24.
- Of shrewdness applied to vicious or cruel ends. 2 Samuel 13:3; 1 Kings 2:9. This was "wisdom" (skill, ability, insight) used for the wrong purposes.

F. *Apparently, "Wise Man" eventually became an official position in Israel.* Jeremiah 18:18. (2 Chron 25:16?)

1. There were "wise men" in other lands: Genesis 40-41; Daniel; Moses and Aaron versus the wise men of Egypt; the wise men of Proverbs; the wise men of Job. See also: Judges 5:29; 2 Kings 6:8; Ezra 7:14-15; Esther 1:13-22; Isaiah 19:11-13; 47:13; Jeremiah 10:7; 50:35; Ezekial 28:2; Obadiah 8; Zechariah 9:2.

2. In Israel: wise women — 2 Samuel 14:2ff; 20:18; advisors — 2 Samuel 16:20ff; "wise men" — Jeremiah 18:18.

G. *Wisdom was not all that was required to please God.*

- Wisdom did not keep one from sinning; see 1 Kings 11:1ff.
- Wisdom could be misused for evil purposes.
- Wisdom could not deliver those whom God had determined to destroy because of their wickedness.

H. *But ideally wisdom was closely related to righteousness.* See Proverbs 1:7; 1:29; 2:1-15, et. al.

I. *Wisdom, while practical, also included a discussion of the greatest questions of the ages*—issues that have always troubled wise men, e.g., the meaning of life and the reason for suffering.

In this respect, it was akin to what would today be called philosophy.

THE BOOK OF PROVERBS

NAME AND CLASSIFICATION

A. The book is named after its first word in Hebrew, a form of the word *Mashal* which is usually translated as "proverb."

- A proverb can be defined as a wise saying; or as a short, pithy, axiomatic saying; or as an epigrammatic saying.
- *Mashal* means something like "a comparison," and is used for types of literature other than what might be called the "pure proverb."

B. Proverbs is classified among the books of Poetry in the English Old Testament, and among the Writings in the Hebrew Bible. It is also one of the books of Wisdom.

AUTHOR AND DATE

A. Authorship:
   1. The book names Solomon (who ruled ca. 970–930 BC) as

the author of many of the proverbs recorded in the book. (1:1; 10:1; 25:1)

2. However, others are said to be "sayings of the wise" (22:17; 24:23) and some are attributed to Agur (30:1) and Lemuel (31:1)—who may not have been Israelites.

3. According to 1 Kings 4:29-34, Solomon was well equipped to write the proverbs in the book. Of course, he may not only have written Proverbs but also have caused them to be written and collected. "Proverbs of Solomon" does not have to mean "authorship."

B. Date:

1. Since, according to 25:1, "the men of Hezekiah" had a hand in copying (and presumably collecting and arranging) some of the proverbs, the book did not reach its final form before 700 BC.

2. Scholars have assigned various dates to the book. LaSor (558) says, "the fifth century is a reasonable date for the final editing."

3. A later date for the final form does not, of course, rule out an early date for much of its contents.

THE NATURE OF THE BOOK

A. It is not like any other book of the Bible in that it contains practical, down-to-earth, good advice, but little about strictly "religious" matters.

B. We should see in it the best example of wisdom in its practical aspect. Perhaps we should see an older man talking with a younger man, giving him advice, telling him how to get along in life, etc. (Notice the "my son" passages: 1:8, 10, 15, 2:1, 3:1, 11, 21; 4:1, 10, 20; 5:1, 7; 6:1, 20; 7:1, 24; 8:32; et al.)

C. Is it then a secular book? No.

- Because all wisdom comes from God. 1:7. In this respect, there is no distinction in the Old Testament between "secular" and "religious."
- Because Proverbs also reveals how to succeed with God. 3:5ff.
- Because, although there is an absence of reference to worship and to Israelite history, the law and the covenant lie behind the moral maxims found in the book.
- Because in this book, wisdom almost equals righteousness. There is no hint here that the wise man might also be an evil man.

INSPIRATION

A. Questions may be raised about the inspiration of the book because of:

- The lack of "religious content" in most of the proverbs.
- Proverbs which speak of things as they are—e.g., 14:35—without recommending righteous or wise behavior.
- The inclusion of proverbs by some who apparently were not Israelites.
- The similarity of some of the proverbs to proverbs that originated in Egypt.

B. But the book can be accepted as inspired:
1. The similarity between the proverbs of Israel and those of other nations merely bears witness to the fact that God delivered His message to the Israelites in forms familiar to the peoples of the ANE.

2. The "non-religious" nature of the proverbs is not significant if:

- It is remembered that all wisdom comes from God.
- If the proverbs are interpreted according to the form in which they are found—as *proverbs*, not as *laws*. If we use the book as God intended us to use it, then we are accepting and respecting it as God's word.

3. The possible inclusion of proverbs by others would suggest that in these cases inspiration involved the selection and editing process—of all the proverbs which could have been chosen, these are the ones the Holy Spirit thought should be included.

4. The book of Proverbs was accepted as God's word by New Testament writers. See, e.g.:

- 1:16 — Romans 3:15
- 3:7a — Romans 12:16, KJV
- 3:11–12 — Hebrews 12:5–11
- 3:34 — James 4:6; 1 Peter 5:5b
- 4:26 — Hebrews 12:13a
- 10:12 — James 5:20; 1 Peter 4:8
- 25:21–22 — Romans 12:20
- 26:11 — 2 Peter 2:22

PURPOSE AND CONTENTS

A. Emphases:

1. Practical. The book emphasizes the practical application of Israel's laws to everyday life.

2. Instruction. The purpose of the book is given in 1:1–7: To instruct both the unlearned and the wise.

3. Key Verse. The key verse is found in 1:7: "The fear of the Lord is the beginning of knowledge..."

4. Theme. Its theme could be said to be: *How a young person can succeed in life.*

B. Outline. The book cannot be outlined according to its subject matter, since it largely consists of disconnected proverbs. It seems, however, to be composed of several different collections of wise sayings. Alden divides it into seven parts based on internal evidence:

- In praise of wisdom — chapters 1:1–9:18.
- The proverbs of Solomon — chapters 10:1–22:16.
- The sayings of the wise — chapters 22:17–24:34.
- More proverbs of Solomon copied by Hezekiah's men — chapters 25:1–29:27.
- The words of Agur — chapters 30:1–33.
- The words of Lemuel — chapters 31:1–9.
- The noble woman — chapters 31:10–31.

INTERPRETATION

A. The book should not be interpreted as if it contained laws like the Ten Commandments.

B. Rather, interpreters should remember the nature of a proverb. A proverb is a general truth—not something that is always 100% true. (See LaSor, 557–58.)

THE BOOK OF ECCLESIASTES

CLASSIFICATION

A. In the English Old Testament, Ecclesiastes is classified as one of the books of Poetry, in spite of the fact that (unlike Job, Proverbs, and Song of Solomon) it is written mostly in prose.

B. In the Hebrew Bible, Ecclesiastes is classified as one of the books of the Writings. Within that category, it is placed (along with Ruth, Esther, Lamentations, and Song of Solomon) among the five little books called the Megilloth which were read at various feasts of the Jews. Ecclesiastes was read at the Feast of Tabernacles.

C. Ecclesiastes is also counted, along with Job and Proverbs, as one of the books of Wisdom. The wisdom tradition in Israel can be divided into two kinds of literature, called by some: (1) "Optimistic"—exemplified by Proverbs (which seems to say, for the most part, that God rewards the righteous with prosperity). (2) "Pessimistic" —exemplified by Job (which asks why the righteous sometimes suffer) and Ecclesiastes (which questions whether anything one does in this life makes any difference anyway).

AUTHOR AND DATE

A. According to tradition, the author was Solomon. Tradition says that Solomon wrote three books:

- Song of Solomon when he was young.
- Proverbs, when he was middle-aged.
- Ecclesiastes, when he was old.

B. The author, although he does not specifically name himself, "sounds like" Solomon, or like someone very much like Solomon.

- See 1:1, 12, 16; 2:3–8.
- There is a long tradition, both in Judaism and in Christianity, that Solomon was the author.
- For arguments in favor of Solomonic authorship and rebuttals of arguments to that position, see Archer, 478ff.

C. There are, however, arguments against this position. LaSor (587–586) gives the following problems with accepting Solomon's authorship:

- Solomon's name is not mentioned in the text.
- Some statements "do not fit well in a king's mouth (e.g., 4:13; 7:19; 8:2–4; 9:14–15; 10:4–7)."
- The book presupposes the highly developed wisdom movement in Israel which cannot be dated before the time of Hezekiah.
- The book's tendency to question the beliefs of ancient Israel points to a time after the peak of prophetic activity had passed.

- Vocabulary and sentence structure seem to be post-exilic.

D. The date of the book depends on the author. If Solomon was the author, then it dates from the tenth century BC; if not, then it is post-exilic (500 BC or later). It has often been dated between 400 and 200 BC.

E. All that can be said is that if the author was not Solomon, it was either someone like Solomon or someone who put himself in the place of Solomon. At any rate, we accept the book as inspired, and the message is the same regardless of who the author was.

TITLE

A. The title "Ecclesiastes" comes from the Septuagint translation and means "The Preacher." (See Eccl 1:1–2.)

B. The Hebrew name for the book is *Qoheleth*, which comes from a verb that means "to assemble." The idea may be "leader of the assembly" or "one who speaks before the assembly."

CANONICITY

There were some doubts as to whether Ecclesiastes belonged in the canon. (LaSor, 586–587)

CONTENTS

A. The theme of the book—announced in Ecclesiastes 1:2 and repeated over and over again-—is "Vanity": "Vanity of vanities, says the Preacher, vanity of vanities! All is vanity." The message is that life is vain—empty—meaningless.

B. Understood in this estimate is that what is under consideration is life "under the sun"—life as experienced by man, life on this earth, leaving God out of consideration, is meaningless.

C. However, since we are destined to spend our life on this earth "under the sun"—and since, in the mind of the writer of Ecclesiastes, suicide is not an option—, we need to spend it in the best way possible. This would include living wisely, working, living happily with your spouse, and enjoying life. This is man's lot.

D. But in the end, in view of the coming of death, of judgment, and of eternity, there is really only one thing that makes man's life meaningful—and that is to serve God acceptably. This is the single major idea that the writer of Ecclesiastes is striving to get across, the conclusion towards which the whole book moves: Ecclesiastes 12:13—"Fear God and keep His commandments; for this is the whole duty of man."

For more information on Ecclesiastes see *Ecclesiastes: A Document Designed to Disturb* by Coy D. Roper (Florence, AL: Cypress Publications, 2022).

THE BOOK OF SONG OF SOLOMON

NAME

A. In the English Old Testament, the book is known as the Song of Solomon, after the first verse of the book.

B. The Greek and Latin versions use the Hebrew title, also from the first verse, Song of Songs, which means "Best of Songs." (*HSB*)

C. It is also called "Canticles," a name derived from the Vulgate.

CLASSIFICATION

A. In the English Old Testament: "Poetry." (A good designation, since it contains some of the finest poetry in the Old Testament.)

B. In the Hebrew Bible: "Writings" —and within that classification, it is one of the five little books called the "Megilloth" and is assigned to be read at Passover.

AUTHOR AND DATE

A. According to tradition, the author was Solomon (who wrote it while he was young).

B. In favor of this view:

- The book is ascribed to Solomon (1:1, 5; 3:7, 9, 11).
- The Bible says that Solomon wrote songs (1 Kgs 4:32).
- Internal evidence favors the view that it was written before the division of the kingdom. (*HSB*)

C. Against this view:

- There are Greek and Persian words in the book, which would suggest a later date—though not necessarily prove it, since the phraseology of the book may have been changed (updated?) by a later editor.
- Other aspects of style seem to point to a later date. (LaSor, 602–603.)
- It is hard to imagine Solomon (with 1,000 wives and concubines) being this much in love with one woman.

CANONICITY

"Acceptance in the Jewish canon did not come easily" (LaSor, 601), probably because of the erotic nature of its contents. But it was eventually accepted when the Jews began to see in the book a picture of God's love for Israel.

INTERPRETATION

A. *What does the book say?* The book obviously is about romantic, erotic, sexual love. Similar poetry about love can be found in the literature of other peoples of the ANE.

1. Solomon figures in this story in 1:1; 3:6–11; 8:11–12. For the kingly setting of the story, see 6:8–9.

2. What do we know about the woman? See 6:13 and 1:5–6.

3. The setting is primarily rural, emphasizing vineyards and shepherds. The story also seems to be set in the North, since the places that are mentioned are in the North of Israel: Gilead (6:5, et. al.), Lebanon and Damascus (7:4, et. al.), Baalhamon (8:11), Heshbon (7:4), Lebanon and Amana and Senir and Hermon (8:8), Engedi (1:14).

4. Several themes run through these love songs:

- The theme of the physical attractiveness of each of the lovers to one another: He describes her (1:10, 15–16; 4:1–7, 9–15; 6:4–9; 7:1–9). She describes him (2:3–4, 8–9; 5:10–16), while she is modest about her own beauty (1:5–6).
- The theme of longing—to be with one another, for the consummation of desire. This is a longing that even causes lovesickness. It is expressed sometimes as a fear of losing the loved one, sometimes by the metaphor of "seeking," sometimes by daydreams involving being with the beloved. See: 1:2; 2:5–6; 2:10–14; 3:1–4; 4:8; 5:2–7, 8; 6:1; 6:11–12; 6:13; 7:8–9; 8:1–2.
- The theme of difficulty—problems stand in the way of the consummation of love. This is implied in the "bad dreams" already mentioned. See also 4:12.
- The theme of acquiesence: the problems are overcome, the longing is satisfied (or will be satisfied). See: 4:16; 5:1; 2:16 (?), 6:2–3; 7:10–14; 8:1, 4–5.

5. From a literary standpoint, perhaps the most outstanding thing about the book is its use of figures of speech, especially similes, and metaphors.

B. *What does the book mean?* Because of its erotic contents, it is hard to know how to interpret the book. Some of the Rabbis at a later date limited the reading of it to mature individuals. Various methods of interpretation have been suggested to get at its meaning; Harrison mentions the following (1052ff):

- Allegorical. If it is interpreted as an allegory: to the Jew, the bride is Israel, the groom is God; to the Christian, the bride is the church, the groom is Christ.
- Dramatic. The book is a drama with two characters—Solomon and the Shulammite woman—and, as in Greek drama, a chorus.
- "Shepherd Hypothesis." A variation on the dramatic approach, this theory sees three people involved in the story. ("Solomon seeks to alienate the affections of the young lady from her lover, but she resists his temptations and the king finally allows her to return home." *HSB*)
- Literal. "The erotic-literary view has seen in Canticles a collection of love-songs or an erotic poem to be understood in its plain and literal sense." (Harrison, 1054)
- Collection of wedding songs.
- Liturgical. Canticles was derived from the liturgical rites of a pagan cult.
- Didactic-moral. "Canticles presents the purity and wonder of true love" … and "teaches the beauty and holiness of the marriage-love relationship that God has ordained for humanity." (Harrison, 1057)

VALUE

If we accept the view that the book is a love song or series of love songs, what value does it have for us? It celebrates romantic, erotic, and sexual love. That love must be expressed in a legitimate relationship, but it is God-given. It has God's approval. It is blessed by Him. (If we did not have this book in our Bible, we might wonder whether this very important part of life is from God.)

MEMORABLE VERSES

A. Some verses have been used in songs and in sermons (and sometimes taken out of context and misapplied):

- 2:1 — "rose of Sharon" and "lily of the valley."
- 2:4 — "banner over me was love."
- 2:15 — "the little foxes."
- 5:10 — "ten thousand."

B. Here are some other memorable verses:

- 1:2 — "Your love is better than wine."
- 1:15 — "You are beautiful my love."
- 4:9–10 — "You have ravished my heart."
- 6:3 — "I am my beloved's and my beloved is mine."
- 8:6 — "Love is as strong as death."
- 8:7 — "Many waters cannot quench love …"

INTRODUCTION TO THE BOOKS OF PROPHECY

CLASSIFICATION

A. In the English Bible, Isaiah–Malachi are classified as prophets.

- Isaiah–Daniel are known as "Major Prophets."
- Hosea–Malachi are known as "Minor Prophets."
- "Major" and "Minor" refer to length, not to the importance of the books.

B. In the Hebrew Bible, the prophets are known as *Nabaaim*.

- The former prophets: Joshua, Judges, Samuel, Kings.
- The latter prophets: Isaiah, Jeremiah, Ezekiel, the Twelve.
- Daniel and Lamentations are classified as belonging to the Writings.

PROPHETS IN THE OLD TESTAMENT

A. There were, in a sense, two types of prophets in the Old Testament.

1. "Oral" prophets. They spoke the word of God, but we have no writings they left.

2. "Writing" prophets. They both spoke the word of God and wrote it, and their writings have been preserved for us.

B. A number of different individuals in the Old Testament are called "prophets."

C. Several words are used to describe the prophets:

- Prophet
- Seer
- Man of God
- Servant of God
- Watchman.

THE PROPHET'S ROLE

A. The prophet was especially called to the task. See the call of Moses, Isaiah, Jeremiah, and Ezekiel.

B. His work was to speak the word of God, to be God's spokesman. His message was: "Thus says Yahweh!" He was God's "mouth." Consider what is revealed about the prophet's work in Exodus 4 and 7, referring to the relationship between Moses and Aaron.

C. Thus, his work was not solely "foretelling" (though this was involved), but "forthtelling." He spoke forth the word of God. He spoke God's word to the people; he was the preacher of his day. He had, first and foremost, a message for his own day.

D. In the sense that his proclamation of that word also declared the consequences of obedience and disobedience, he also spoke of the future even when he spoke to the people in the present.

E. The prophet also spoke sometimes of events in the far distant future. There are prophecies of the coming Messiah and His kingdom, though the New Testament says that sometimes the prophet himself did not understand what he was saying.

F. In addition, the prophets spoke to the nation as a whole, since Israel was God's covenant people. In this sense, they were involved in affairs of state.

G. There were other prophet-like figures in the ancient Near East, but there are more differences than similarities between them and Israel's prophets.

'TRUE' AND 'FALSE' PROPHETS

A. There were false prophets, apparently of two types.

B. How could you tell the difference?

- The false prophets tended to say what their listeners wanted to hear. See, e.g., the case of Micaiah and the 400 false prophets. (1 Kgs 22) (Notice that the question was: Did the prophet speak from Yahweh? The true prophet did; the false prophet didn't.)
- The prophet was a false prophet if his prophecies or "signs" did not come true. See Exodus 4:8; Deuteronomy 18.
- A prophet who spoke in the name of a false god was a false prophet. Even if the signs of a prophet did come true, he was a false prophet if his teachings contradicted what had previously been revealed. See Deuteronomy 13:1–3.

EVALUATIONS OF THEIR WORK AND IMPORTANCE

A. Some have thought that they are the real originators of the religion of Israel, that they were religious geniuses who originated the idea of ethical monotheism. *Against this view*, it can be said that, while they are important, they are not the originators of the Law. *They did not claim to be the originators of anything; rather, they called the people back to the Law of Moses.*

B. Some have thought that they were completely uninspired and spoke only to their own generation. *Against this view: they claim to speak of the future also and to speak by the inspiration of God.*

C. Some have thought that they were religious geniuses, who, although they did not originate the religion of Israel, nevertheless had such insight into the law, the world, and mankind, that they could predict what would happen, by natural, not supernatural, means, if people persisted in their present behavior. This view says that they also spoke to the future, as well as to the present. *Against this view, it should be remembered that they claimed to speak by the inspiration of God.*

D. The best view is to see them as God's spokesmen, speaking by inspiration from God, primarily to their own generation, but also of what would happen in the future.

THE PROPHETS CHARACTER

Consider Elijah, Elisha, Nathan, Micaiah, e.g. They were individualistic, strong, courageous, and fanatically loyal to Yahweh, but human.

THE PROPHETS MESSAGE

EHB: (1) The ruler of all history. (2) The primary need to be right with God. (3) The moral foundation of religion and society. (4) A blend of judgment and hope. (5) The messianic kingdom.

A. The prophets often had a message of doom: Israel is to be destroyed. (But other nations were also to be destroyed because of their sin.)

B. But there was also a thread of hope running through the prophets: After the destruction, there will be a revival, a restoration. Or by repentance, Israel could avert the destruction.

C. There was also a call for righteous living and for repentance.

D. There is, in addition, an important Messianic hope for the future in the prophets: "Someone is coming."

THE PROPHETS AND THE NEW TESTAMENT

INTERPRETING THE PROPHETS

(See John Willis, *My Servants the Prophets*, Vol. 1, 23–24; Jack Lewis, *The Minor Prophets*, 8–9; Samuel Schultz, "Interpreting the Prophets," in *The Literature and Meaning of Scripture*, ed. by Morris Inch and C. Hassell Bullock, 105–110.)

A. The prophets spoke from God. (See 1 Pet 1:20–21.)

B. It is most important to remember that the prophets had a message for their own day. Any interpretation which would have meant *nothing* to the original readers is probably wrong.

C. In studying a specific passage, it is most important first to understand the message of the entire book, then to ask how the passage under consideration fits into the book and contributes to its message.

D. It is extremely important to notice the context in which the prophet spoke. Who speaks in each passage? To whom?

About what? For what purpose? What is the "speaker's tone of voice"? What is the historical setting of the particular passage?

E. The prophets, for the most part, prophesied around the time of the Assyrian crisis and captivity and around the time of the Babylonian crisis and captivity. Destructions predicted in the prophets probably refer to the destructions brought upon Israel by Assyria and Babylon. Generally, the prediction of coming glory probably refers to the return from Babylonian captivity.

F. One must also consider the literary form used in a specific passage. Is the passage prose or poetry? A taunt song? Does the writer employ irony? Does the writer speak directly, or use figurative language? The prophets often used figurative language to get their point across (it may even be a kind of "prophetic language"). Therefore, one must be careful not to understand all their words as if literal language is being used.

G. The prophets did speak of the future and of the Messiah and His coming kingdom. (See Acts 3:24–26; Rom 1:2.) And sometimes, according to the New Testament, they themselves did not understand what they were saying. (See 1 Pet 1:10–12.) *But the only way we can know for sure that a specific prophecy refers to Christ or to the church is that the New Testament says so.* (See Heb 1:1–2.)

H. It is a defensible position to assert that most, if not all, of the Old Testament prophecies concerning the Christ were fulfilled in His first coming and in the establishment of the church, and that few, if any, were left to be fulfilled after the end of the first century AD.

I. Sometimes prophecies (predicting the future) had both a "near" and a "far" fulfillment. See Isaiah 7 and Matthew 1.

J. Prophecy is conditional. Sometimes the apparent non-fulfillment of the prophecy is the result of conditions being, or not being fulfilled. (See Jonah.)

THE MESSAGE OF THE PROPHETS

THE PROPHETS INSISTED THAT THEY SPOKE FROM GOD

A. Jeremiah 1:9 — "I have put my words in your mouth."

B. Amos 7:14–15 — "The Lord said to me, 'Go, prophesy ...'"

C. See also: Isaiah 1:10; Ezekiel 13:1; Zephaniah 1:1; Zechariah 1:1; Hosea 1:1; Micah 1:1; Nahum 1:12; Joel 1:1; Obadiah 1:1; Jonah 1:1; Malachi 1:1; Habukkak 1:1.

THE PROPHETS PRESENTED AN IMPRESSIVE PORTRAIT OF GOD

A. He is living; and is, in fact, incomparable. Isaiah 40:18–31; 44:6–20.

B. He is glorious beyond description. Isaiah 6:1–5; Ezekiel 1:28.

C. He reigns over all creation, including all the nations, not just Israel. Jeremiah 27:5–6; Daniel 2:37; 4:25–26; 5:18–23.

THE PROPHETS PREDICTED THAT DESTRUCTION WAS COMING!

A. This fact was pointed out by many, or most, of the prophets.

- Jeremiah 7:15 — "I will cast you out of my sight ..."
- Amos 7:11 — "Israel must go into exile away from his land."
- Hosea 1:4 — "I will put an end to the kingdom of ... Israel."
- See Jeremiah 5:15–17; Ezekiel 5:8; Amos 4:12; Zephaniah 2:4–15; Jonah; Nahum; Obadiah; Micah 4:10.

B. The coming destruction was sometimes spoken of as the "day of the Lord."

- Zephaniah 1:14–15 — "The great day of the Lord is near ... a day of wrath ... of ruin."
- See Isaiah 13:6, 9; Jeremiah 46:10; Ezekiel 30:3; Amos 5:18–20; Joel 2:1.

C. Although other nations would be the source of the destruction, God was using them as His instruments to punish His people. Jeremiah 27:5–6 — "It is I who by my great power ... have made the earth ... and I give it to whomever it seems right to me. Now I have given all these lands into the hand of Nebuchadnezzar ..."

D. The destruction will come because of sin (especially sins of social injustice and idolatry).

- Jeremiah 7:9 — "Will you steal, murder, commit adultery, swear falsely, burn incense to Baal, and go after other gods ..."

- Hosea 4:1–19 — "There is swearing, lying, killing, stealing, and committing adultery (v. 2) ... Ephraim is joined to idols. (v. 17)"
- See Micah 1:3–5; 2:1–2; Zephaniah 1:2–6; Zechariah 7:12–14; Amos 1–2.

E. While God would punish the nation, individuals were accountable only for their own sins. Ezekiel 18:20 — "The soul that sins shall die."

F. Israel's privileged status would not save it from destruction. Jeremiah 7:4 — "Do not trust in these deceptive words: 'This is the temple of the Lord, the temple of the Lord, the temple of the Lord.'"

THE PROPHETS URGED THE PEOPLE TO REPENT AND LIVE RIGHTEOUSLY

A. Repentance was essential:

- Isaiah 1:16ff — "Wash yourselves; make yourselves clean; remove the evil of your doings ... cease to do evil, learn to do good ..."
- Hosea 14:1 — "Return, O Israel, to the Lord your God."
- See Jeremiah 26:13; Amos 5:4–6; Jonah; Zephaniah 2:3; Joel 2:12–14.

B. Righteous living, and not just ritual, was called for.

- Isaiah 1:13 — "Bring no more vain offerings ... I cannot endure iniquity and solemn assembly."
- Amos 5:21–24 — "I hate, I despise your feasts, and I take no delight in your solemn assemblies ... But let justice roll down like waters, and righteousness ..."
- See Micah 6:6–8; Amos 4:1–5; Zechariah 7:8–10.

THERE WAS HOPE FOR THE FUTURE

A. A remnant would be saved.

- Zephaniah 3:12–13 — "For I will leave in the midst of you a people humble and lowly."
- Micah 2:12 — "I will gather the remnant of Israel ..."
- See Micah 4:6–7; Amos 3:12.

B. Blessings awaited Israel when Israel returned from bondage.

- Micah 7:18–20 — "Who is a God like thee, pardoning iniquity ... He will again have compassion upon us ..."
- Hosea 14:4–7 — "They shall return and dwell beneath my shadow."
- See Joel 3:17; Amos 9:14–15; Zechariah 8:3ff; Joel 3:1; Zephaniah 3:14ff.

C. The prophets also spoke of the Messianic age.

- Isaiah 53 — "He has borne our griefs ..." (1 Pet 2:24, et al.)
- Jeremiah 31:31ff — "I will make a new covenant ..." (Heb 8:8–12)
- Joel 2:28ff — "I will pour out my spirit on all flesh ..." (Acts 2)
- Amos 9:11–12 — "I will raise up the booth of David." (Acts 15)
- See Isaiah 2:1ff; 7:14 (Matt 1:23); Micah 4:1ff; Malachi 4:5 (Matt 11:14, et al.); Micah 5:2 (Matt 2).

THE PROPHETS OFTEN HAD A PRACTICAL MESSAGE FOR THEIR OWN PEOPLE

A. Haggai 1:8 — "Go up to the hills and bring wood and build the house."

B. See Zechariah 1:16; Malachi 3:10.

THE PROPHETS ALSO HAD A MESSAGE CONCERNING OTHER NATIONS

A. Doom will come upon other nations because of their sins. See Isaiah 13–23; Jeremiah 46–51; Ezekiel 25–32; Obadiah; Nahum; Amos 1–2; Jonah.

B. But they also speak of the nations serving or worshiping God. See Isaiah 2:1–4; 56:3ff; Malachi 1:11.

CHRONOLOGY OF THE PROPHETS[1]

THE CANONICAL PROPHETS

Eighth Century Prophets

Joel — 800 BC (?)[2]
   Jonah — ca. 782 BC
   Hosea — 745 BC
   Amos — 760 BC
   Isaiah — 740–680 BC
   Micah — 735 BC–696 BC

Seventh Century Prophets

Nahum — 625–612 BC
Zephaniah — 630–622 BC
Jeremiah — 627–585 BC
Habakkuk — 608 BC

Exilic Prophets

Daniel — 605–530 BC
Ezekiel — 593–570 BC
Obadiah — 586 BC (?)[2]

Post Exilic Prophets

Haggai — 520 BC
Zechariah — 520–518 BC
Malachi — ca.435 BC

ENDNOTES

[1] These dates are taken from a number of sources and should be considered only approximate.

[2] There is no consensus among scholars as to the dates of Joel and Obadiah.

OTHER BIBLICAL PROPHETIC PERSONAGES[3] WITH APPROXIMATE DATES

Abraham — Genesis 20:7 — nabi' — 2000 BC
 Moses — Deuteronomy 18:15 — nabi' — 1200 BC
 Aaron — Exodus 7:1 — nabi' — 1200 BC
 Miriam — Exodus 15:20 — nabi' — 1200 BC
 Eldad & Medad — Numbers 11:26-27 — "Prophesied" — 1200 BC
 (Balaam — Numbers 22-24 — no title!) — 1200 BC
 Deborah — Judges 4:4 — nebi'ah — 1100 BC
 Anon. — 1 Samuel 2:23 — 'is 'elohim — 1075 BC
 Samuel — 1 Samuel 9:9 — ro' eh — 1050-1010 BC
 Samuel — 1 Samuel 3:20 — nabi' — 1050-1010 BC
 Band of prophets — 1 Samuel 10:10 — nebi'im — 1020 BC
 Saul — 1 Samuel 10:12 — nabi' — 1020 BC
 Gad — 1 Samuel 22:5 — nabi — 1000 BC
 Gad — 2 Samuel 24:11 — hozeh — 980 BC
 Nathan — 2 Samuel 7:2 — nabi — 990 BC
 Heman — 1 Chronicles 29:30 — hozeh — 970 BC
 Asaph - 2 Chronicles 29:30 — hozeh — 970 BC
 Jeduthun — 2 Chronicles 35:15 — hozeh — 970 BC
 Ahijah — 1 Kings 11:29f — nabi — 930 BC
 Shemaiah — 2 Chronicles 12:5 — nabi — 917 BC
 Anon. — 1 Kings 13:1-10 — nabi — 915 BC
 Iddo — 2 Chronicles 9:29 — hozeh — 900 BC
 Azariah — 2 Chronicles 15:8 — ? — 890 BC
 Jehu — 1 Kings 16:1-4 — nabi' — 890 BC
 Hanani — 2 Chronicles 16:7, 10 — ro'eh — 877 BC
 Anon. — 1 Kings 20:13ff — nabi' — 860 BC
 Anon. — 1Kings 20:28 — nabi' — 860 BC
 Sons of prophet — 1 Kings 20:35 — 860 BC
 Micaiah b. lmlah — 1 Kings 22:8-20 — 860 BC
 Elijah — 1Kings 17-19 — nabi' — 855 BC
 Elisha — 2 Kings 2-9, 13 — nabi' — 845 BC

Sons of prophets — 2 Kings 2:3; 9:1 — 845 BC
Anon. — 2 Chronicles 25:16 — nabi' — 790 BC
Jonah b. Amittai — 2 Kings 14:25 — nabi — 770 BC

ENDNOTES

[3] Adapted from a handout by Professor George Mendenhall, University of Michigan. Dates given before the Monarchy reflect a different view of Old Testament history than those found elsewhere in this book.

THE BOOK OF ISAIAH

ISAIAH'S TIMES

A. He lived during the days of the following kings: Uzziah (783–742 BC), Jotham (742–735 BC), Ahaz (735–715 BC), Hezekiah (715–687 BC). He is thought to have died during the reign of Manasseh (697–642 BC). Tradition says he was sawn in two. (See Heb 11.)

B. The year that King Uzziah died (Isa 6:1) was 742 BC; Sennacherib died in 681 BC, about five years after Hezekiah's death (Isa 37:38; 2 Chron 32:32). Isaiah probably prophesied for sixty years.

C. He lived during the days of the Assyrian threat. Tiglath Pileser Ill (Pul) was involved with Judah in the Syro-Ephraimite war about 734 BC (Isa 7:1–9; 2 Kgs 16; 2 Chron 28:16–21). During his ministry, the Assyrian king Shalmaneser conquered the Northern Kingdom of Israel and deported its people (during the days of Hoshea, king of Israel, and about 722 BC—see 2 Kgs 17). Also, during his career the Southern Kingdom of Judah was threatened by the Assyrian king Sennacherib (about 701 BC—see 2 Kgs 18:9–19:37; 2 Chron 32:1–23; Isa 36:37).

D. He lived in the Southern Kingdom of Judah during the days of the Divided Kingdom. He was closely connected with the kings of Judah—especially Ahaz (Isa 7) and Hezekiah (Isa 36–37).

E. He lived in the capital city of Jerusalem—unusual for a prophet, for the prophets were mostly from small towns. Tradition has it that Amoz was the brother of Amaziah; thus Isaiah might have been of royal blood. Certainly, he had easy access to the throne.

F. He had a wife (Isa 8:3) and two sons (Isa 7:3; 8:1). Notice their names!

G. He was a great man: poet, prophet, statesman, advisor, orator, writer.

H. His name means Salvation of Yahweh.

ISAIAH'S CALL: ISAIAH 6

- the vision of the holiness of God,
- the prophet's reaction: a realization of his own sinfulness,
- the prophet's cleansing,
- the Lord's call,
- the prophet's response,
- the Lord's commission.

OUTLINE OF THE BOOK

A. Isaiah 1–39 — warning — for Judah and other nations.
  B. Isaiah 40–66 — comfort. See Isaiah 40:1–2.

MAIN EMPHASIS

ISAIAH IS THE MESSIANIC PROPHET! He speaks, perhaps more than any other prophet, of the coming Christ, the Messiah.

OF SPECIAL SIGNIFICANCE

A. Isaiah 1—the spiritual state of God's people, God's view of sacrifice.
    B. Isaiah 2, 9, 11—the coming kingdom.
    C. Isaiah 7—Immanuel, questions of translation and the interpretation of prophecy.
    D. Isaiah 7–12—God, Judah, Israel, and Assyria—see 7:4, 16–17; 10:5–7, 25.
    E. Isaiah 13ff—prophecies against the nations.
    F. Isaiah 30:1–5—warning against seeking help from Egypt.
    G. Isaiah 36–39—historical section.
    H. Isaiah 40:1–2—comfort.
    I. Isaiah 42, et al.—the "servant" prophecies.
    J. Isaiah 53—prophecies concerning the Messiah.
    K. Isaiah 55, 61, 62—various prophecies.

QUESTIONS OFTEN ASKED

A. The unity of Isaiah: What about "second" and/or "third" Isaiah?
    B. The "Servant Songs": Who is the servant?

MEMORY VERSES

1:18; 2:2; 7:14; 9:6; 53:4–5; 59:1–2; 62:2.

NOTES ON THE UNITY OF ISAIAH

THE QUESTION BEING DEALT WITH IS WHETHER THERE WAS ONE ISAIAH, OR TWO OR THREE. TO DEFINE THE ISSUE MORE EXACTLY:

A. The traditional view is that Isaiah, who lived in the 8th century BC, wrote the entire book of Isaiah. This view is still held by most conservative scholars.

B. Some scholars a hundred years ago or so ago decided (for reasons given below) that the book of Isaiah is not a unity, but is, in reality, two books. They divided the book into two parts: First Isaiah (written by the historical Isaiah in the 8th century BC), chapters 1–39; and Second (or Deutero) Isaiah, chapters 40–66, written sometime during the Babylonian Exile, by an unknown author in Babylon.

C. Since then other scholars have decided that the last part of Isaiah was written by another author; thus, they divide the book into three parts: First Isaiah (1–39), Second Isaiah (40–55), Third (or Trito) Isaiah (56–66).

D. The division of the book continues. Liberal scholars think they find, even within these major parts, various other sources by different authors. The final book was then the result of the work of a *redactor* (or editor).

E. So the opinion of many liberal scholars is that in Isaiah you have:

1. Isaiah's words,
2. plus later additions,
3. plus the work of redactors,
4. accomplished over a long period of time.

F. The aim of the critical scholar is to try to define to which strata of the work each passage belongs, and then to explain the passage in terms of why and when it was added.

G. This is the most important critical question that is raised when dealing with the book of Isaiah.

WHAT DIFFERENCE DOES IT MAKE WHETHER ISAIAH IS A UNITY OR NOT? MUST WE BELIEVE THAT ISAIAH OF JERUSALEM (8TH CENTURY BC) WROTE THE WHOLE THING?

A. Most conservatives are willing to grant that some editing took place, or some things were inserted at a later date, and—for some books—that documents were used in putting together the final edition of the book.

B. And it is possible to believe that God guided the editing process.

C. It should also be noted that if Second Isaiah is a different book, the prophet who wrote it could have been inspired. God can inspire an anonymous prophet. We accept various books in the Bible as inspired, even though they are anonymous (e.g., Hebrews, and the historical books of the Old Testament).

D. The biggest problem involved in attributing part of the book to another author is that the New Testament attributes the entire book to Isaiah. Compare Matthew 3:3 and Isaiah 40:3; Matthew 4:14–15 and Isaiah 9:1,2; Matthew 8:17 and Isaiah

53:4; Matthew 12:17–18 and Isaiah 42:1–4; Matthew 13:14 and Isaiah 6:9–10; Romans 10:20 and Isaiah 65:1; John 12:38–41 and Isaiah 53:1 as well as Isaiah 6:9–10.

E. Thus, conservatives would usually say that to believe in the Second Isaiah is to disbelieve in the New Testament.

F. Is it possible for us to attribute any part of the book to someone else if the New Testament attributes it to Isaiah? Perhaps, by assuming that the attributions in the New Testament are to a work named "Isaiah," rather than to the 8th-century prophet Isaiah. (See below.) But the safest course seems to be to think of it as the work of Isaiah of Jerusalem.

WHY BELIEVE THAT ISAIAH IS COMPOSED OF TWO OR THREE BOOKS?

A. It seems unlikely, unreasonable, and illogical, that a specific prophecy concerning Cyrus would have been made 150 years or so before Cyrus ever lived. See Isaiah 44:28 and 45:1. To the liberal this would have to be a prophecy-after-the-fact.

> This passage presents some difficulties for Bible believers. Whereas the prophets frequently make predictions, their predictions are not usually this specific. Jeremiah foretold the return in 70 years but didn't mention that it would be accomplished by Cyrus. Habakkuk foresees that the Chaldeans will destroy Judah, but he doesn't mention names. In Amos 3:11, Amos speaks of "an adversary," but doesn't mention which adversary. This is more typical.

B. The setting for the second part of the book seems to be different from that of the first.

- The first part has to do with the threat from Assyria, the second with that from Babylon.

- The writer of the second part seems to be writing from within the exile; Childs: "The historical setting of chs. 40ff. reflects the exilic period because Jerusalem is pictured as having fallen and the captives deported."

C. The second part of Isaiah does not seem to speak to a specific need of the people of Isaiah's day. Unlike Amos and Hosea, Isaiah 40–66 lacks particularity.

D. There are striking differences in style, language, theme, and subject matter. "Deutero-Isaiah" dwells upon the infiniteness of God, e.g., and upon the suffering servant. (See Archer, updated and rev. ed., 1994, 384.)

ANSWERS TO THESE ARGUMENTS

A. Regarding Cyrus:

1. Rejection of this prophecy may indicate an anti-supernatural bias.
2. Predicting by name is unusual, but not altogether unknown. In 1 Kings 13:2, a prophet predicted that Josiah would destroy the idolatrous altar at Bethel; this was fulfilled almost 300 years later.

B. Regarding the different setting:

1. The setting is not Babylonian. The geography, names of plants, etc., in the latter part of the book are Palestinian.
2. Even if it were, there is no reason why the prophet could not be transported into the future, and so prophesy as if he were living in exilic times.

C. Regarding the lack of a message in Isaiah 40–66 for 8th-century readers: There was a message, but it was about the future as well as the present. See 41:26; 42:9, 23; 43:9, 12; 44: 7–8. See also 8:16. How did this benefit the first readers? In the same way that knowing about heaven benefits you!

D. Regarding differences in style, etc.:

1. Differences are exaggerated.
2. They don't prove anything; the same writer can stress different things, use a different style, etc., at different times, according to a changing maturity, changed purposes, etc.

ADDITIONAL ARGUMENTS FOR THE UNITY OF ISAIAH

A. It was considered just one book by Jews and Christians. The Dead Sea Scrolls (100 BC?) include a copy of Isaiah without any break between Isaiah 39 and 40.

B. The futility of the other approach: What does it accomplish?

1. Scholars cannot agree on the sources.
2. There is a large measure of subjectivity, and guesswork in their attributing a passage to one source or another.
3. After they have finished, they must still deal with the text as it is; the text as it is is the only concrete reality we have.

C. The setting of Isaiah 40–66 in some ways better fits pre-exilic times: e.g., in the mention of idolatry—44:9–20; 56:4–5; 57:7; 65:2–4; 66:17.

D. "A most formidable difficulty is presented to the Deutero-Isaiah theory by the fact that the author's name was not preserved." (Archer, 349). And this author is often thought to be the greatest of the writing prophets!

OTHER EXPLANATIONS, MEDIATING POSITIONS

A. LaSor suggests that the mention of Isaiah's disciples (Isa 8:16) may be significant. Perhaps these disciples kept Isaiah's teachings alive, and in the spirit of Isaiah added to them as the years went by. Isaiah died ca. 685 BC. There could have been disciples alive who knew Isaiah personally at the time Babylon arose. (Notes by LaSor)

B. Childs says that Second Isaiah was really written by someone else, but not in opposition to First Isaiah, nor to try to sneak something in another's name, but to show how Isaiah's prophecies in the first part of the book were fulfilled. This author considered his book merely a continuation of the first book, not a different work, but a part of the same one. Childs even ventures a guess that the two books *never* circulated separately.

C. Regarding the New Testament attribution to Isaiah: Willis says that this can be taken as quoting from a book named "Isaiah," without regard for who was the author of the book.

WHAT SHALL WE CONCLUDE?

A. There is no compelling reason to accept the idea of two or three Isaiahs.

B. We are safe if we simply refer to what we find in the book as having been said by Isaiah.

SELECTED BIBLIOGRAPHY

Allis, Oswald T. *The Unity of Isaiah: A Study in Prophecy.* Philadelphia: The Presbyterian and Reformed Publishing, 1950.

Archer, Gleason L. *A Survey of Old Testament Introduction.* Chicago: Moody, 1964.

Childs, Brevard. *Introduction to the Old Testament as Scripture.* Philadelphia: Fortress, 1979.

Gilmer, Richard A. "The Isaiah Polemic." Unpublished paper; Rochester, MI: Michigan Christian College, 1981.

Harrison, Roland Kenneth. *Introduction to the Old Testament.* Grand Rapids, MI: Eerdmans, 1969.

Thomas, J. Harold, "The Authorship of the Book of Isaiah," *Restoration Quarterly.* (1967) 46–55.

Wood, Leon J. *The Prophets of Israel.* Grand Rapids, MI: Baker Book, 1979.

Young, Edward J. *The Book of Isaiah.* 3 vols. Grand Rapids, MI: Eerdmans, 1969.

————. *Who Wrote Isaiah?* Grand Rapids, MI: Eerdmans, 1958.

THE BOOK OF JEREMIAH

NAME

The book is named after its author—the prophet Jeremiah.

CLASSIFICATION

In the English Old Testament, Jeremiah is one of the Major Prophets; in the Hebrew Bible, the book is classified among the Latter Prophets.

AUTHOR

A. Interesting facts about Jeremiah (DR):

- He contributed more to the Old Testament than any other writer except Moses.
- The book of Jeremiah is the second largest in the Bible (next to Psalms)—1/20 of the Bible (Isaiah — 37,000 words; Jeremiah — 42,000 words).
- There is more biographical material on Jeremiah than on any other character, even David.

B. Biographical information:

1. Jeremiah was the son of Hilkiah, from Anathoth, a city of priests—and Hilkiah was a priest. He was, therefore, a "small-town boy," as were most of the prophets.

2. Jeremiah prophesied about 627–587 BC, for more than 40 years.

3. He was called to be a prophet as a young man. In chapter 1 can be seen:

- God's choice of the prophet.
- The prophet's reluctance: "I am only a youth."
- God's commission and assurance.
- The prophet's mission.

4. He continued to serve his people throughout the period during which they were threatened, attacked, and destroyed by Babylon. After the final destruction of Jerusalem, he had the opportunity to go to Babylon and live as a privileged guest. He refused and was taken to Egypt by rebellious Jews. He may have died there.

5. He served during the reigns of the last five kings of Judah: Josiah (640–609), Jehoahaz (609), Jehoiakim (609–598), Jehoiachin (598), and Zedekiah (598–587). All of these kings were "bad," except for Josiah. (Gedeliah was the governor who served after this.)

6. Two major events during his ministry were: Josiah's reform and the beginning of the Babylonian Captivity. The book does not mention Josiah's reform.

7. During his career he was frequently abused:

- The men of Anathoth plotted against him — chapter 11.
- Pashur had him beaten and put into stocks — chapter 20.

- He was threatened with death — chapter 26.
- He was opposed by false prophets — chapters 27–28.
- He was imprisoned in Zedekiah's court — chapter 32.
- His words were burned by Jehoiakim — chapter 36.
- He was thrown into prison by Zedekiah — chapter 37.
- He was thrown into a cistern — chapter 38.
- Rebellious Jews refused his advice — chapters 42–44.

8. He failed in his attempt to get the people to repent. Because of the abuse and this failure, he sometimes felt like quitting. See 20:7–9. But he couldn't because of his "call."

DATE

Jeremiah prophesied between about 627 BC (the 13th year of Josiah's reign) and 587 BC (the approximate date of the destruction of Jerusalem). What he said was written down during his lifetime, much of it by Baruch, his scribe.

HISTORICAL SETTING

The reigns of the last five kings of Judah, the destruction of Judah, the destruction of Jerusalem and the temple by Nebuchadnezzar, and the deportation of the Jews to Babylon provide the historical background of the book.

OUTLINE (FROM *HSB*)

A. Prophecies under Josiah and Jehoiakim — chapters 1:1–20:18.

B. Prophecies under Jehoiakim and Zedekiah — chapters 21:1–39:18.

C. Prophecies after the fall of Jerusalem — chapters 40:1–45:5.

D. Prophecies against heathen nations — chapters 46:1–51:64.

E. Historical appendix — chapters 52:1–34.

PURPOSE, EMPHASIS, MESSAGE

A. Emphasis: Jeremiah is known as "the weeping prophet." (Jer 9:1) This is probably not an altogether fair designation. Jeremiah wept because of the coming destruction of Judah.

B. Jeremiah's Message:

- Judgment is coming: The Babylonians. See 15:1–2; 5:15–17; 6:22–26. But Babylon will later be destroyed.
- Judah's sins were to be the cause of her destruction. See 4:15–19; 5:32; 23; 7:1ff; et. al. Especially did Judah's refusal to repent contribute to her downfall. See 8:5.
- The people should repent. See 4:1–2; 7:1–7; 26:17. It was still not too late.
- Since destruction is coming, Judah should submit to Babylon. See 27–28, 38. This advice was the issue between Jeremiah and the false prophets.
- There is hope: Judah would return from exile in 70 years. See 5:18–19; 29:10–14; 30:1–3. Ultimately, God would make a "new covenant." See 31:31–34.

JEREMIAH AND THE NEW TESTAMENT

A. Jesus was thought to be like Jeremiah.

B. The "new covenant" passage is quoted in Hebrews 8.

C. The slaughter of the children—31:15.

MEMORABLE PASSAGES
1:5; 5:1; 6:13–14; 6:16; 7:4; 20:9; 31:31–34.

THE BOOK OF LAMENTATIONS

FACTS ABOUT LAMENTATIONS

A. It was thought to have been written by Jeremiah. One outline on Lamentations is headed "Jeremiah weeps again." However many scholars doubt that Jeremiah is the author.

B. It is classified among the Major Prophets in the English Bible, probably because Jeremiah is thought to be the author. This probably also determines its place in the Old Testament, following Jeremiah.

C. It is classified as among the Writings in the Hebrew Bible. Specifically, it is one of the Megilloth (Scrolls)—five little books within the category "Writings" (*Kethubim*, or Hagiographa), each of which is read at a different feast day of the Jews. Lamentations is read at "Tisha b'Ab" (the black fast)—on the 9th day of the 4th month (corresponding to our July), the anniversary of the destruction of Jerusalem.

D. It is a series of dirges (funeral songs), lamenting (expressing great sorrow) over the destruction of Jerusalem. Thus, the historical background of the book is the conquest of the nation of the Jews, the deportation of the Jews, and, especially, the destruction of the city of Jerusalem by the Babylonians about 587/586 BC. It is worth noting that other lamentations over the destruction of cities in the ANE are known.

E. Perhaps most interesting is the form these lamentations take. Each chapter is a separate poem. *And the first four poems are acrostic poems.* An acrostic poem is one in which the first line of the poem begins with the first letter of the alphabet, and each succeeding line begins with a succeeding letter of the alphabet. Since there are 22 letters in the Hebrew alphabet, there are 22 lines in each of these acrostic poems, except for chapter three, which has 66 verses, and every third verse begins with a succeeding letter of the Hebrew alphabet. Though the last poem in the book is not acrostic, it, too, has 22 lines. Why did the writer use this form? Consider: Why do some poets write limericks? Others, sonnets? Also, see below.

CONTENTS

The book contains —

A. A description of the destroyed city — 1:1, 4–5; 2:11–12, 15, 21; 4:7–10; et al.

B. The cause of the fall:

- The people's sins — 1:8–9, 14, 18–19; 4:22; 5:7; et al.
- The leaders' sins — 1:19; 2:14; 4:13; et. al.
- God — 1:18; 2:1–8; 2:17; 4:16; et. al.

C. The prophet's reaction — 1:12, 16, 20; 2:11; 3:1ff, 49; et al.
D. Advice to the remaining Jews — 3:21–32.
E. Appeals to God — 1:20–22; 3:49–51, 58–66; 5:1–22.

MEMORABLE VERSES

1:1; 3:22–24; 3:31–33; 3:40–42.

SIGNIFICANCE

A. *Eerdmans Handbook to the Bible*:

> To the people of Judah, the fall of the city meant more than the loss of their beautiful and almost unassailable capital. It was more than just the destruction of a nation's capital city. His temple was there. This was where God chose to live with his people. And when Jerusalem was burned, the temple destroyed, the people deported, they knew that God had given them up to the enemy. It could not have happened otherwise. So these laments express the poet's grief, not simply over the suffering and humiliation of his people, but over something deeper and far worse, that God had rejected his people because of their sin. (414)

B. H. L. Ellison, *The Message of the Old Testament*:

> The most striking feature of the book is that the first four poems show an alphabetic acrostic ... The purpose was probably to keep the writer's overflowing grief and anguish within bounds, while containing the suggestion that here we have the whole of human grief portrayed from A to Z. ... God was well pleased to recognize that men can be overwhelmed by grief even while they continue to trust in Him, and so He permitted the expression of that grief to find its place in Scipture. [Some] may readily claim that we should rejoice in the Lord at all times ... The facts of human experience show, however, that the clouds of grief may settle down on the choicest of saints ... It is then that Lamentations comes into its own. It does not clear the clouds, but it does assure the mourner that God understands and accepts his grief. (81–82)

THE BOOK OF EZEKIEL

NAME

Named after its author, the prophet Ezekiel.

CLASSIFICATION

In the Hebrew Bible: "Latter Prophets." In the English Old Testament: Major Prophets.

AUTHOR

A. The book was written by the prophet Ezekiel.

1. A priest and the son of Suzi (1:3); his name means "God will strengthen."
2. He was taken captive with Jehoiachin in 597 BC (33:21; 40:1).
3. He lived among the exiles by the river Chebar, which was probably a canal (1:1–2); probably he lived in the town of Telabib (3:15, 24); he had his own home (8:1),

and was married until his wife died, at which time he was not allowed to weep (24:15–18). *He prophesied from Babylon.*
4. He was a younger contemporary of Jeremiah. Daniel was already in Babylon when Ezekiel arrived there, although Daniel would have been a little younger than Ezekiel.
5. He was thirty years old when he began prophesying in 592 BC (1:2), and continued his work until at least 571 BC (29:17). *Tradition says that he died in Babylon.*

B. Some liberal scholars:

1. question the unity of the book,
2. believe that Ezekiel may have had some sort of mental problem that caused him to see the kind of visions the book records. Their arguments are not convincing.

DATE

Ezekiel's prophecies are dated from about 592 BC to about 571 BC.

HISTORICAL SITUATION

Judah had existed as a kingdom for 140 years after the destruction of Israel. But the Jews refused to learn from Israel's punishment and became as guilty of sins as Israel had been. Consequently, God sent the kingdom of Babylon against Jerusalem and Judah. The Babylonians attacked and conquered Judah at least twice, and then in 587 or 586 BC Nebuchadnezzar invaded and conquered Judah, destroyed the temple, and deported the Jews to Babylon. Ezekiel was one of those taken into exile sometime before the final destruction of Jerusalem.

The Babylonian Conquest and the Exile provide the background for this book.

OUTLINE (FROM DR)

A. Before the destruction of Jerusalem, Judgment on Judah — chapters 1–24.

B. During the siege and destruction, prophecies against the nations — chapters 25–32.

C. After the destruction, comfort for Judah — chapters 33–48.

PURPOSE, MESSAGE, METHOD

A. Ezekiel's purpose apparently was to provide what the Jews needed at specific times during his ministry.

1. First: His aim was to guard against undue optimism. Apparently, before the Babylonian conquest (which occurred about 587/586 BC), the Jews were overly optimistic because

- they were Abraham's seed,
- a descendant of David was still on the throne, and
- the temple, with God's name, still stood.

To meet that need, Ezekiel was first a preacher of doom.

2. Second: His aim was to guard against undue despair. In the latter part of the book, Ezekiel promises revival and restoration. See Ezekiel 37. He then becomes a preacher of comfort.

3. Between these two points are messages of doom to the nations, which also meet a need in the life of God's people.

B. Ezekiel's message is like that of the other major prophets, but his method often differs. EZEKIEL IS THE VISIONARY PROPHET.

1. His writing is something like *apocalyptic literature*. *HSB* says that apocalyptic literature is characterized by symbols and figures like: "supernatural events, unearthly creatures, metaphors, pseudonyms, and numbers." *EHB* speaks of such literature as being "… poetic and visionary, expressing its meaning through symbols and imagery." Thus, Ezekiel is like Daniel and Zechariah in the Old Testament, and like Revelation in the New Testament. Examples: Ezekiel 1, 37, 38, 39.
2. The book is characterized by Ezekiel's use of "visual aids," vivid imagery, and figures of speech.

C. Harrison says that Ezekiel emphasizes:

1. Divine transcendence, in contrast to Jeremiah, who emphasized Divine immanence.
2. The moral responsibility of the individual; see Ezekiel 18.
3. That the triumph of restoration was that God would be in the temple; the final three words of the prophecy are: God is there.

EZEKIEL AND THE NEW TESTAMENT

Ezekiel has a special affinity with Revelation; compare 1:5 and Revelation 4:6; 1:7 and Revelation 1:15; 2:18; et al.

MEMORABLE PASSAGES

3:17–19; 18:20; 18:30–32.

THE BOOK OF DANIEL

CLASSIFICATION

A. In the English Old Testament, Daniel is classified as one of the major prophets. See also Matthew 24:15.

B. In the Hebrew Bible, Daniel is classified among the writings. Why? (Rather than Prophecy?)

- Daniel contains little in the way of moral exhortation. See Daniel 4:27.
- Daniel, though a righteous man, may not have been known as a prophet.
- Possibly, the canon of prophecy was already complete when the book was written.

WHO WAS DANIEL? HE WAS THE PROPHET OF THE CAPTIVITY

A. See Daniel 1:1–7. He was born in Judah, taken to Babylon before 600 BC, and among the first of the captives (the "best" were taken first). He was prepared by his captors for service in the king's bureaucracy. He was given a Babylonian name: Belteshazzar.

B. He lived in Babylon through the reigns of the following:

- Babylonian Kingdom (to 539 BC). Kings: Nebuchadnezzar, (Nabonidus), Belshazzar.
- Medea-Persian Kingdom. Kings: (Cyrus), Darius the Mede.

C. He attained prominence in these kingdoms, through his interpretation of dreams, his faithfulness to God, and his good work. He served two kingdoms and three kings faithfully.

D. He lived to a ripe old age (he would have been about eighty when he was cast into the lions' den), beyond the time when the first Jews returned to Palestine. He died about 533 BC.

THE BOOK

A. Author: According to tradition, it was written by Daniel himself. An alternative theory says it was written during the Maccabean period during the 2nd century BC. But this idea is based, at least in part, on an anti-supernatural bias. (See Daniel 11.)

B. Language: The book is unusual in that it was written partly in Hebrew, and partly in Aramaic, the official language of the day.

C. Contents: The book divides neatly into two parts:
1. The first six chapters — A HISTORICAL SECTION:

- Four young men, and the food incident. (Why would they not eat?) — chapter 1.
- Nebuchadnezzar's dream and Daniel's interpretation — chapter 2.

- The golden image and the fiery furnace — chapter 3.
- Nebuchadnezzar's insanity — chapter 4.
- Belshazzar's feast, and the writing on the wall — chapter 5.
- Darius and Daniel in the lion's den — chapter 6.

2. The second six chapters — A VISIONARY SECTION:

- Vision of four beasts. (See ch. 2.) — chapter 7.
- Vision of the ram and the he-goat — chapter 8.
- Daniel's prayer and Gabriel's answer: seventy weeks — chapter 9.
- A vision of the last days — chapters 10–12.

D. Style: Much of Daniel, especially the second section, is written in the style of *apocalyptic literature.* Revelation and Daniel are closely related.

PURPOSE

A. The purpose of Daniel's career: Perhaps God provided Daniel, in His providence, to make life in captivity easier for the Jews.

B. The purpose of the book of Daniel:

1. To give the Jews assurance that there was coming a time when the kingdoms of the earth would come to nothing, but God's kingdom would stand forever. (See Dan 2.)
2. To assure the Jews of that day, and of future generations, that God would be with them in times of tribulation if they would be faithful to Him. (See Dan 1, 3, 6.)

3. To demonstrate to the Jews that Yahweh is greater than any heathen god.
4. Possibly, to be used by the Jews as they proclaimed their faith to Gentiles.
5. To provide both good examples and bad examples.

MEMORY VERSES

2:44; 3:17–18; 6:5; 6:10.

SPECIAL QUESTIONS

A. Does Daniel teach there will be a premillennial kingdom?
B. Why is Daniel written partly in Aramaic?
C. When was Daniel written?

OVERVIEW OF THE MINOR PROPHETS

PROPHET: PERSONAL SITUATION – HISTORICAL SITUATION – MESSAGE

This chapter provides the following overview of each of the Minor Prophets: his personal situation, his historical situation, and his message. Fuller details are given in the chapters that follow.

Hosea
— Name's meaning: Salvation. Northern Kingdom. Son of Beeri; Wife: Gomer (harlot). Three children.
— Before Assyrian captivity. Uzziah, Jotham, Ahaz, Hezekiah (Judah); Jeroboam (Israel). 8th cent.
— Israel will be destroyed because of her sins. GOD'S LOVE FOR FAITHLESS ISRAEL

Joel
— Name's meaning: Yahweh is God. Southern Kingdom. Son of Pethuel

— Unknown. Locust plague.
— Repent! 2:28 = Acts 2. BETTER DAYS COMING!

Amos
— Name's meaning: Burden. From the Southern Kingdom spoke to the Northern Kingdom. Fr. Tekoa, shepherd & farmer. "Not a prophet."
— Before Assyrian captivity; Jeroboam II's reign; prophesied at Bethel. 8th cent.
—Israel is to be destroyed because of her sin. SINS OF ISRAEL

Obadiah
— Name's meaning: Servant of Yahweh. Southern Kingdom. Unknown.
— Unknown. After the destruction of Judah.
— 1 ch. Destruction of Edom. VIOLATION OF BROTHERHOOD

Jonah
— Name's meaning: Dove. Northern Kingdom. 2 Kings 14:25. Of Amittai. Reluctant prophet. Unhappy at repentance.
— Reign of Jeroboam II. Israel prospered; Assyria was her enemy. 8th cent. Time of Writing: ?
—Prophet's story is message: SHARING GOD'S LOVE FOR THE NATIONS

Micah
— Name's meaning: Who is like Yahweh? From Moresheth, Southern Kingdom

— Before Assyrian Captivity. Joham, Ahaz, Hezekiah. 8th cent.

— Judgment, both Kingdoms. WHAT DOES THE LORD REQUIRE?

Nahum

—Name's meaning: Consolation. Southern Kingdom, From Elkosh.

— Before fall of Nineveh, ca. 620 BC. 7th cent.

— Nineveh's fall. DOOM COMES AT LAST!

Habakkuk

— Calls himself a prophet. Preached in Judah.

— Prophesied just before Babylonians conquered Judah. 7th cent.

— Why is evil unpunished? Why do evil men win? PROBLEM OF EVIL

Zephaniah

— Name's meaning: Whom Yahweh has hidden. Related to kings. Preached in Judah.

— Just before the Babylonian conquest. Josiah's reforms. 7th cent.

— Judah destroyed, a remnant remains. THE DAY OF THE LORD!

Haggai

— Name's meaning: Festive. Aim: Finish the temple. Cf. Ezra 5–6. Judah. Prophet of return.

— Rebuilding begun: 536 BC. Haggai, Zechariah began 520 BC. Job finished: 516 BC.

— Practical message: Build the Temple! FIRST THINGS FIRST!

Zechariah

— Name's meaning: Whom Yahweh has remembered. Son of Berechiah. Worked with Haggai

— People were few, poor, subjugated to Persians, without hope.

— Comfort. (1:13) Apocalyptic. EIGHT COMFORTING WORDS.

Malachi

— Name's meaning: Messenger. Prophet of restoration, last prophet of the Old Testament. Judah.

— Related to Ezra, Nehemiah (similar concerns). 5th cent.

— Sins: sacrifice, tithes, priesthood, marriage. ROBBING GOD.

THE BOOK OF HOSEA

CLASSIFICATION, AUTHOR

A. Hosea is the first, and one of the longest, of the minor prophets.

B. The book is named after its author, the prophet Hosea, whose name means "Salvation" and is related to the root word for "Joshua."

C. Hosea is identified as the "son of Beeri." He prophesied to the Northern Kingdom, Israel.

HISTORICAL SETTING

A. *Hosea's work is set towards the end of the period of the Divided Kingdom in the eighth century BC.*

B. He prophesied during the reigns of Uzziah, Jotham, Ahaz, and Hezekiah, kings of Judah, and during the reign of Jeroboam II, king of Israel (other kings of Israel are not mentioned, though they probably reigned during his lifetime). His prophetic ministry has been dated from ca. 760 to ca. 720 BC.

C. He was a contemporary of Amos, who also prophesied to

the Northern Kingdom, and of Isaiah and Micah, who were prophesying about the same time in the Southern Kingdom.

D. He lived and worked, therefore, during the twilight years of Israel, the Northern Kingdom.

1. The kingdom had been divided when Rehoboam succeeded Solomon as king over all Israel, about 930–920 BC.
2. The two Kingdoms—Israel and Judah—existed side by side for about two hundred years.
3. Then the Northern Kingdom was captured and its people taken away into captivity by the Assyrians about 722 BC. They never returned from that captivity. The Southern Kingdom was also in danger of being destroyed at about the same time but was finally delivered by God. (See 1:6–7.)

E. Signs of weakness in Israel were plentiful from about 740 BC on. But it is probable that, at the time that Hosea wrote, the Northern Kingdom was strong and felt secure. (See 8:14; 10:1; 10:13; 12:8.)

OUTLINE

A. Hosea's relationship with his wife is a type of God's relationship with Israel — chapters 1–3.

B. Israel has sinned (been unfaithful to God), and God will punish Israel for those sins unless Israel repents — chapters 4–13.

C. A restoration is promised — chapter 14.

MESSAGE

A. The emphasis of Hosea is: *God's love for faithless Israel*.

1. God teaches that message, especially by using Hosea's life as a kind of object lesson.

- At God's direction, Hosea marries a prostitute named Gomer. (1:2) He has three children by Gomer; their names indicate his message to Israel: a son named Jezreel, a daughter named "Not pitied," and another son named "Not my people." (1:3–9)
- Apparently Gomer then becomes an adulteress. God instructs Hosea to bring her back into his house. (3:1–5)

2. The love Hosea showed towards Gomer is like the love God has for His faithless people Israel.

B. Recurring themes in the book:

1. Israel had forsaken God by deliberately refusing to hear or obey the law of God. "My people are destroyed for lack of knowledge." (4:6)

2. They had sinned against God and man.

- They were guilty of idolatry.
- They were guilty of many sins against their fellow man: no kindness, lying, murder, stealing, adultery, drunkenness, greed, deceit, et al.
- Their leaders were also sinful.

3. They had—sinfully and uselessly—depended on other people and things rather than on God.

- They had made or attempted to make, alliances with other nations, specifically Assyria.

- They had depended on their arms and fortifications.

4. Consequently, they were destined for destruction.
5. God did not want to destroy them, for He loved them.
6. Neither was their destruction inevitable. If Israel would return to God, God would restore Israel.

SIGNIFICANT QUESTIONS

The major question raised by the book of Hosea has to do with Hosea and his wife Gomer.

A. Is the story about Hosea and Gomer a historical narrative or a parable?

B. If it is historical, what happened? Was Gomer a prostitute when God first spoke to Hosea, or did she become one later? Do chapters 1 and 3 represent two different times when Hosea took Gomer to be his wife?

THE BOOK OF JOEL

NAME, AUTHOR

A. The book is named after its author, the prophet Joel.

B. Joel's name means "Yahweh is God." He was the son of Pethuel (1:1).

C. He was a prophet of Judah. (See 3:1 and the mention of the "house of the Lord" and of Zion.)

DATE

A. There is no certainty about the time of Joel's prophecy.

- *HSB*: "Many conservatives hold that the internal evidence supports the pre-exilic view that it was written before 800 BC."
- Others prefer a date in the sixth century BC.
- Still, others have set the date in the fifth century. Harrison, e.g., dates the book a little before 400 BC.

B. The message is the same whenever the prophecy was given.

HISTORICAL SETTING

A. Since there is no consensus as to the time the book was written, the political situation of Israel at the time of writing is disputed.

B. The occasion for writing, however, is undisputed: it was a devastating locust plague. (1:4ff) This is interpreted by God's prophet as a judgment by God on His people, which requires repentance on the part of the people.

PURPOSE(S)

A. To help God's people understand that the "natural catastrophe" of the locust plague was God's judgment on them.

B. To motivate Judah to repent.

C. To provide promises, both near and distant, to encourage Judah.

OUTLINE

A. The locust plague: God's past and present judgment — chapters 1:1–2:11.

B. The call to repentance and its desirable consequences — chapter 2:12–27.

C. The future: blessings and judgment — chapters 2:28–3:21.

OF SPECIAL SIGNIFICANCE

A. Peter quotes Joel 2:28–32 on the Day of Pentecost (Acts 2:17ff), saying that Pentecost fulfilled the Joel prophecy.

B. Other memorable passages:

- Joel 2:12–13 — It would be difficult to put the challenge to repent in a more impressive way.
- Joel 3:14 — "Multitudes, multitudes in the valley of decision!"

THE BOOK OF AMOS

NAME, CLASSIFICATION, IMPORTANCE

A. The book is named after its author, the prophet Amos, whose name means "burden" or "burden bearer."

B. Although the book is classified as one of the "minor prophets," it is not minor in importance. Amos is credited with being one of the greatest prophets; he is thought by many to be the first of the canonical prophets, and thus to be a kind of prototype for others.

HISTORICAL SITUATION

A. Amos was a prophet of the 8th century BC. He prophesied during the Divided Kingdom during the days of Uzziah (Azariah — 2 Kings 15:1ff), King of Judah (783–742 BC), and Jeroboam II, King of Israel (786–746 BC). Most would date his ministry around 750 BC.

B. He prophesied at the time that Assyria was the greatest nation in the area and was threatening Israel and Judah. Within a few years (ca. 722 BC), Assyria conquered Israel and deported the Israelites.

C. He was originally a farmer and shepherd. (7:14–15) He was from Tekoa (1:1), which is six miles southeast of Bethlehem, and in the Southern Kingdom.

D. He did not claim to be a prophet (7:14), which suggests that he did not hold "professional" prophets in high regard. Yet he was called to prophesy. (7:15) His reaction to God's call is exemplary.

E. Although he was from the Southern Kingdom, his message was for the Northern kingdom (1:1), and he was sent to Bethel to deliver it. (7:10–16) His message to Israel seemed to involve speaking against the king and against the altar at Bethel (7:13) and predicting the exile of the nation of Israel. (7:11, 17)

F. His message was not well received by Amaziah, the high priest at Bethel, who told him to go home to Judah. (7:12–13) Amos replied by predicting Amaziah's exile. (7:17)

OUTLINE

A. The book can be divided into three parts (Willis, *My Servants the Prophets*, vol. 1, 52):

1. Oracles against the nations. Including oracles against Judah and Israel — chapters 1–2.
2. Oracles against the sins of Israel — chapters 3–6.
3. Five visions. Including Amos's encounter with Amaziah in Bethel — chapters 7–9.

- Locusts (7:1–3)
- Fire. (7:4–6)
- Plumbline. (7:7–9)
- Basket of summer fruit (8:1–3)
- Lord beside the altar. (9:1–10)

B. Lewis says,

> It is not uncommon for a prophetic book to have three elements: (a) oracles against nations, (b) oracles of doom for Israel, and (c) oracles of hope. The book of Amos has each of these elements. (17–18)

EMPHASIS

The main burden of Amos is that judgment is coming upon Israel because of her sins.

A. Israel's situation was:

- She was rich and at ease. (3:15; 4:1; 6:1, 4)
- She was religious; there was no neglect of religious forms. (4:4–5; 5:21–24)
- Israel believed God was with them and trusted in that relationship. (5:14; 9:10)

B. But the sins of Israel were many:

- They were guilty of sexual sins. (2:7)
- They had mistreated the righteous and the poor. (2:6–7; 5:11)
- They had accepted bribes. (5:12)
- They had been dishonest in business. (8:5–6)

C. All that God had done to bring about repentance had not worked.

- Israel would not listen to the prophets. (2:11–12; 5:10)
- The calamities God had sent had not produced repentance. (4:4–12)

D. Repentance was still required. (5:4, 6, 14–15, 24)

E. But Amos also seemed to say that it was too late to repent: judgment was coming! (5:1–2; 6:14; 5:27; 7:11, 17; 5:18) Almost the whole of the land would be destroyed; only a remnant would remain. (3:12)

F. Yet there would come a time when David's tabernacle would be rebuilt. (9:11–15) This was fulfilled in New Testament times; see Acts 15.

MEMORABLE VERSES

4:12; 5:21–24; 6:1; 7:14–16a.

THE BOOK OF OBADIAH

THE PROPHET AND HIS BOOK

A. The prophet's name means "Servant of Yahweh." Nothing else is known about him.

B. The book is the shortest in the Old Testament, containing only one chapter, consisting of only 21 verses.

HISTORICAL SETTING

A. The book refers to a destruction of Jerusalem (v. 11). Since Jerusalem was attacked and overcome several times in Old Testament history, besides the final destruction in 587/586 BC, there is no way to be certain which of these events in particular occasioned the prophecy. There is, therefore, considerable uncertainty concerning the date of the book. *For our purposes, it is assumed that the destruction spoken of is related to the Babylonians' capture of the city.*

B. Edom was a nation descended from Esau and, therefore, related to Israel. It was one of Israel's closest neighbors. However, a state of hostility or war often existed between the two lands. The Edomites became known as the Idumeans in the period between the Testaments, and from them were descended the Herods of Jesus's day. After the destruction of Jerusalem in AD 70, they disappeared from history.

C. A number of other prophets also predict the destruction of Edom: See, for example, Isaiah 34:5–17; Jeremiah 49:7–22; Ezekiel 25:12–14; Joel 3:19; Amos 11:11–12.

THE MESSAGE

A. The theme of the book of Obadiah is: *the destruction of Edom because of Edom's mistreatment of Israel*. In giving emphasis to the destruction of a people other than Judah or Israel, Obadiah is like the book of Nahum, and unlike most of the other prophets.

B. What had Edom done?

1. Specifically:

- They had done violence to Jacob. (v. 10)
- They stood aloof. (v. 11)
- They were like Jacob's enemies. (v. 11)
- They gloated, rejoiced, and boasted over Judah's ruin. (v. 12)
- They entered the gates and looted Jerusalem after the battle. (v. 13)
- They cut off Judah's fugitives. (v. 14)

2. Basically, they had failed to act as a brother should have acted!

C. What was to happen?

- Edom was to be destroyed. Nothing would be left. This day of destruction is called in v. 15 "the day of the Lord."
- Nothing could help Edom.

D. In contrast, Judah would be restored.

THE APPLICATION OF THE MESSAGE TO TODAY

A. God was (is) God of all nations. He calls each to account for its actions and condemns unrighteousness, violence, and cruelty wherever it is found.

B. One of the major sins for which nations are condemned is their mistreatment of God's people.

C. God's rule is: "As you have done, it shall be done to you, your deeds shall return on your own head." (v. 15)

D. When God makes up His mind to destroy a nation, there is no way that nation can escape.

E. And especially: *To fail to act towards others as brothers should act is a sin*!

THE BOOK OF JONAH

NAME

A. The book of Jonah is named after its main character, the prophet Jonah, whose name means "dove."

B. Jonah was the son of Amittai. 2 Kings 14:25 identifies him as being from Gath-Hepher (which was just north of Nazareth) and as living during the time of Jeroboam II, in the early part of the eighth century BC.

AUTHOR, DATE

A. The book of Jonah differs from other prophetic books in that it does not claim to be written by the prophet Jonah; rather, it is a book about Jonah. Jonah's prophetic message consists of only a few words. *The message of the book is the story about Jonah.*

B. However, even though Jonah is not identified as the author of the book, he has traditionally been accepted as the one who wrote down the record of the incidents it records.

C. Others believe that the book dates to a period of time later than the eighth century BC.

D. In weighing the evidence, it should be remembered that the time when the events of the book occurred and the time when they were put into book form do not have to coincide. In other words, it is possible that the events occurred about 780 BC, but the book was not written until long afterward.

HISTORICAL SETTING

A. Jonah is told to go prophesy against Nineveh. Nineveh was the capital city of Assyria, the greatest power of the ANE at the time the events recorded in the book occurred. In practical terms, that means that Assyria was Israel's enemy. More than that: Assyria used terror as a policy of state; it was perhaps the most bloodthirsty, cruel regime that history had known.

B. Jonah at first refused to go, setting sail for Tarshish instead (going in the opposite direction).

C. But a storm at sea, being cast overboard to die, and spending three days in the belly of a great fish, changed his mind.

D. He went to Nineveh and proclaimed the message God had given him—namely, that God was going to destroy Nineveh. But the people of Nineveh repented and God spared the city.

E. Rather than making Jonah happy, these results saddened and depressed him. The book ends with God's attempt to get Jonah to be happy that Nineveh had been spared.

OUTLINE

A. Jonah's attempt to flee from God and from his responsibility and the consequences of that attempt — chapter 1.

B. Jonah's prayer in the belly of the fish and his deliverance — chapter 2.

C. Jonah's successful mission to Nineveh — chapter 3.

D. Jonah's reaction to Nineveh's repentance — chapter 4.

PURPOSE

A. Several things are taught in the book of Jonah:

- One cannot get away from God.
- A prophet must not shirk his mission.
- Why a prophet's prediction may not come true.
- Even the most sinful person or nation can repent, and, if he or it does, God will forgive.

B. But the main lesson seems to be: *Israel should share God's love and concern for other nations.*

SIGNIFICANT QUESTIONS

A What is the date of the book?
    B. Can the "fish story" be accepted as true?
    C. Is the book history, parable, or allegory?

JONAH AND THE NEW TESTAMENT

Jesus's preaching is compared to Jonah's and the time He spent in the tomb is compared to the Jonah spent in the belly of the fish. (Matt 12:38–41)

THE BOOK OF MICAH

AUTHOR, DATE

A. The book is named after its author, the prophet Micah. Micah's name means "Who is like God?"

B. He was from Moresheth, which was near Gath and about thirty miles from Jerusalem. Thus, he was a prophet of the Southern Kingdom, Judah, during the period of the Divided Kingdom.

C. He prophesied in the latter part of the eighth century BC during the reigns of Jotham, Ahaz, and Hezekiah, kings of Judah. He was a contemporary of Isaiah, and possibly of Amos and Hosea.

D. His writing shows a close relationship to that of Isaiah (cf. especially Micah 4 and Isaiah 2), although, unlike Isaiah, he seems to have had no connection with the court or with state politics. It may be that what Isaiah preached in the city (of Jerusalem) Micah preached in the countryside.

AUDIENCE ADDRESSED

Unlike any other of the minor prophets, the book of Micah is a prophecy that is specifically addressed to both the Northern and Southern Kingdoms: "The word of the Lord ... concerning Samaria and Jerusalem." (1:1)

HISTORICAL SETTING

A. During the eighth century BC, within the period of the Divided Kingdom, both the Northern and Southern Kingdoms were threatened by the great empire of Assyria.

B. Micah's task was to predict judgment against both Israel (1:6–7) and Judah (3:12)—a judgment that would come upon them deservedly because of their sins.

C. This prediction of judgment was intended to bring about repentance. Israel did not repent, and so was destroyed about 720 BC. Judah, in contrast, did repent—at least Hezekiah repented (see Jer 26:16–19)—and was spared.

OUTLINE (FROM DR)

A. God's judgment to fair ... — chapters 1–3.
   B. In the midst of this, Messianic hopes ... — chapters 4–5.
   C. A plea for repentance ... — chapters 6–7.

PURPOSE

A. To pronounce judgment against both Israel and Judah.
   B. To predict a brighter future.

EMPHASES

A. Micah speaks against the political, business, and religious leaders of the day: against the rich (2:1–2; 6:12), against crooked businessmen (6:10–11), against rulers (3:1–4, 9–12; 7:3), against false prophets (3:5–7, 11), against priests (3:11).

B. Micah emphasizes the total sinfulness of the people. There are no godly men left (7:2ff). Those who hear him are unwilling to give heed to his words (2:6–7, 11).

C. Micah stresses the primary requirements we must fulfill to please the Lord. (6:6–8)

D. Although Micah is a prophet of doom, he holds out some hope.

- He speaks of a restoration and of a remnant.
- He also speaks of a wonderful age to come. (4:1–4) This is usually thought to be a prophecy of the Messianic age.
- Micah 5:2 speaks of the place where the Messiah would be born.
- Israel's hope for the future was based on God's nature. (7:18–20)

THE BOOK OF NAHUM

THE PROPHET

The prophet's name means "consolation," "comfort," "relief," or "comforted by Yahweh." (LaSor) He is from Elkosh, but no one knows where Elkosh was located.

THE HISTORICAL SETTING

A. The book was written while Assyria was still—as it had been for most of about two hundred years—the most powerful nation in the Near East. About the middle of the seventh century, it reached the zenith of its power and ruled a vast empire. It established a pattern of empire building and control that was followed by all the empires that followed. Assyria had earlier (722 or 721 BC; see 2 Kings 17) conquered the Northern kingdom of Israel and almost destroyed Judah (2 Kgs 19). However, Assyria was defeated by the Babylonians and Medes, and Babylon eventually took over the empire.

B. Nineveh is referred to in the prophecy, but Nineveh stands for Assyria since it was the capital of the empire.

C. The book must have been written between 663 BC, when No-amon or Thebes, of Egypt, was sacked by Ashurbanipal of Assyria (an event referred to in 3:8–10), and 612 BC when Nineveh was destroyed. Probably it should be dated in the latter part of that fifty-year period—perhaps about 620 BC.

CONTENTS

A. Message: The Destruction of Nineveh!
   1. The book differs from many of the other prophets in that:

   - It does not rebuke Judah for its sins, nor require Judah to repent.
   - It is (like Obadiah, but unlike most other prophets) primarily about what will happen to a nation other than the Jews.

   2. The destruction of Nineveh is presented in vivid terms.
   3. The reason for the destruction is not elaborated at great length; basically, it seems to be found in 3:1ff. Assyria was known for its violence and cruelty.
   4. Nineveh's destruction will bring comfort to Judah. Furthermore, others will be glad; no one will grieve at her destruction. See 3:5–7, 9.
   5. The destruction of Nineveh did, in fact, come; the predictions of Nahum were fulfilled. So complete was the desolation that the site of Nineveh was not identified until AD 1845.

B. Purposes:

   - To bring comfort to Judah. See 1:12–13, 15; 2:2. (The prophecy would not have been heard by the Assyrians.)
   - To teach what God is like. See 1:2ff.

MESSAGE FOR TODAY

"At Last ... Judgment Comes." The story of Jonah is also about Nineveh. But then (perhaps 770 BC—maybe 150 years earlier), Nineveh repented and was spared. But Nineveh returned to its violence and cruelty, and "at last" God did to Nineveh what He had purposed to do in Jonah's day. "The Lord is slow to anger and of great might" ... but eventually He will destroy the wicked ... He then "will by no means clear the guilty." (1:3)

THE BOOK OF HABAKKUK

THE PROPHET

Nothing is known for certain about the author except his name. His name may derive from an Assyrian word which signifies a vegetable or a plant. (*HSB*)

HISTORICAL SETTING

Habakkuk prophesied not long before the Babylonians destroyed Judah, thus in the last part of the seventh century BC, perhaps about 605 BC. He would probably have been a contemporary of Zephaniah, Jeremiah, and Nahum, though we have no record of his having a long ministry, as did Jeremiah.

MESSAGE

A. The book deals with the problem of evil. Other Old Testament passages also deal with this question, but Habakkuk approaches the issue differently.

    B. Habakkuk differs from other prophetic books in that:

- Habakkuk speaks to God (presumably on behalf of man) rather than speaking to man on behalf of God. However, it is probable that the message was intended to teach the people of Judah.
- Habakkuk uses a question/answer (dialogue) method, asking God questions and then recording His answers.

OUTLINE

A. First Question: How long will it be until God punishes the evil in Judah? (1:1–4)

B. God's Answer: God will send the Chaldeans (Babylonians) to punish Judah. (1:5–11)

C. Second Question: Is it right to use a wicked nation to punish a nation that is less wicked? (1:12–17; 2:1)

D. God's Answer: The wicked will be destroyed, but the righteous will live by their faith. (2:2–20)

E. Habakkuk's Response: Since God is all-powerful and all-good, Habakkuk will accept whatever happens. (3:1–19)

MEMORABLE PASSAGES

1:4, 13; 2:4, 14, 19–20; 3:2 ("In wrath remember mercy."); 3:17–18.

THE BOOK OF ZEPHANIAH

THE PROPHET

A. His name means: "he whom Yahweh has hidden or protected."

B. He was descended from Hezekiah, thus of royal blood, a prince as well as a prophet, and related to Josiah. In this, he differed from most of the other prophets. (See 1:1.)

C. He prophesied during the reign of Josiah (640–609 BC). Freeman (*An Introduction to the Old Testament Prophets*, 233–234) argues that the book must be dated before Josiah's reforms in 621 BC because the situation as described in 1:3–6, 8–9, 12, and 3:1–7 fit the situation before the reform better than the situation after it.

THE HISTORICAL BACKGROUND

A. Assyria had reigned supreme in the ANE for almost two hundred years before the days of Josiah and had apparently reached its zenith about 650 BC. However, Assyria collapsed within a generation after that, and Babylon inherited its empire.

B. Evidently the fall of the Northern Kingdom was intended to serve as a warning to the Southern Kingdom. God sent no prophet, after Isaiah, after the fall of Israel. However, Judah did not learn the lesson it was intended to learn from Israel's fall. Very soon Judah, under the wicked king Manasseh and his son Amon, lapsed into idolatry and other sinful practices, and prophets again were sent—Zephaniah, Habakkuk, and Jeremiah. This may also illustrate that prophets arise in times of crisis.

C. During Zephaniah's life the reforms of Josiah are carried out. (See 2 Chron 34 and 2 Kgs 22–23.) It may be that Zephaniah played a part in motivating Josiah to instigate these reforms. The reform didn't "take", and Judah was destroyed by Babylon.

ZEPHANIAH'S MESSAGE

A. Basically, Zephaniah's message was: The Day of the Lord is Coming! Other prophets had also spoken of the Day of the Lord. (See Obad 15; Joel 1:15; Amos 5:18–20.) But Zephaniah's book seems to be altogether about it. The nature of the day:

1. Imminent. 1:14.

2. Terrible. 1:15. Notice also 1:7. What was to be the sacrifice?

3. Day of judgment because of sin. 1:17. Of what were they guilty?

- Idolatry. Including seeking to worship both idols and the Lord, and failing to inquire of the Lord. 1:4–6.
- Violence and fraud. 1:9.
- Crooked business dealings. (?) 1:10–11.
- Self-satisfaction and practical atheism. 1:12–13.
- Failure to trust in or to draw near to God. 3:1–2.

- Bad leadership. 3:3–5.
- Refusal to repent. 3:6–7.

4. Universal, upon all creation, man and beast, Jew and Gentile — 1:2–3; 2:4–15; 3:8.
5. Severe, as only a remnant will survive — 2:3, 7, 9; 3:9–13.

B. Outline:
1. The Day of Wrath for Judah — 1:2–2:3.
2. The Day of Wrath for the Nations — 2:4–15.

- For what are the nations to be destroyed? They have taunted Israel (2:8); they have been prideful — 2:10, 15.
- What will be the result? They will bow down to the Lord — 2:11.

3. The Day of Wrath for Jerusalem — 3:1–8.
4. Hope for the Future — 3:9–20.

C. Purposes of the book:
1. To warn of the coming "Day of the Lord"—upon Judah and all nations.
2. To inspire repentance. See 2:3 and 3:6–7. It was not too late.
3. To predict restoration.

OF SPECIAL SIGNIFICANCE

The concept of the "Day of the Lord." What does it mean here and elsewhere in the prophets? It sounds as if there will be complete destruction—1:18 and chapter 2—, but Judah will not be completely destroyed (2:7, 9; 3:9; 3:12) and will eventually be restored. Notice 3:20—other nations do not cease to exist.

MEMORABLE VERSES

1:7; 1:14; 2:3; 3:9.

THE BOOK OF HAGGAI

CLASSIFICATION

Haggai is classified in the English Old Testament as one of the minor prophets and in the Hebrew Bible as one of "The Twelve," and part of the Latter Prophets.

NAME, AUTHOR, DATE

A. The book is named after its author, the prophet Haggai.

B. Haggai's name means "Festival" or "Joyous One," indicating that he may have been born on the day of a festival.

C. He was one of two prophets (the other is Zechariah) mentioned in the book of Ezra who encouraged the Jews to complete the rebuilding of the temple after their return from Babylonian captivity. (Ezra 5:1; 6:14)

D. Four oracles are included in the book. All are dated by the prophet himself and were delivered in the year 520 BC.

STYLE

A. Haggai is written in prose, rather than poetry. It could be said that his style appears rather dull and prosaic; he speaks plainly, directly, and briefly.

B. With only 38 verses in two chapters, Haggai is the second shortest book of the minor prophets. (The shortest is Obadiah, with only one chapter.)

HISTORICAL SETTING

A. Because of the sins of Judah, God used Babylon to punish His people. Babylon had conquered Judah, destroyed Jerusalem, destroyed the temple, and taken the Jews away into captivity about 587 or 586 BC. The policy of deportation was practiced by both the Assyrians and the Babylonians, apparently to reduce the risk of successful rebellion on the part of captured peoples.

B. The prophets had predicted that the Jews would be allowed to return to their own land after 70 years.

C. In accordance with that promise, after the Babylonian Empire fell to the Medes and Persians, the Persian king Cyrus the Great—in keeping with his general practice towards captive peoples—issued a decree that allowed the Jews to return to Palestine.

D. About 50,000 Jews returned under the leadership of Sheshbazzar and Zerubbabel in about 538 BC. (Ezra 1–2) After that return, the first order of business was the rebuilding of the temple. The rebuilding began; the foundation of the temple was laid to the accompaniment of both tears and rejoicing. (Ezra 3) Opposition then arose from the people who were in the land, and the project stopped. (Ezra 4)

E. In 520 BC, at the urging of the prophets Haggai and Zechariah, rebuilding began again. (Ezra 5) The temple was finally completed, in large part due to the work of these two prophets, about 516 BC. (Ezra 6)

F. The book of Haggai contains the message of Haggai which helped encourage the people to complete the task.

MESSAGE

A. Haggai has but one message: Build the Temple! (1:8)

B. There is, therefore, no denunciation of social injustice, immorality, or idolatry in the book. (Lewis, 68)

OUTLINE

A. First oracle (1:1–15): Your present distress has resulted from putting your own business before the Lord's business (building His house).

B. Second oracle (2:1–9): Don't let your unpromising beginnings discourage you and keep you from the work of building.

C. Third oracle (2:10–19): Your work in the past yielded few results, but from now on it will be blessed.

D. Fourth oracle (2:20–23): Take comfort from the fact that God will destroy the nations that are your enemies and that you have a leader chosen by God.

MEMORABLE PASSAGE

1:5–11. Lesson to be learned: *Put First Things First!*

THE BOOK OF ZECHARIAH

NAME, AUTHOR, CLASSIFICATION

A. The book is named after its author, the prophet Zechariah, whose name means "remembered by Yahweh."

B. He identifies himself as "the son of Berechiah, the son of Iddo, the prophet." (1:1) He may be the same man who is identified in Nehemiah 12:16 as a priest. He is thought to have been a young man at the time the book was written. (2:4)

C. The book is obviously divided into two parts. Chapters 1–8 differ markedly in style from Chapters 9–14. This has led many to suppose that Zechariah 9–14 was written by someone else and at a different time from the first eight chapters. Others, accepting the unity of the book, account for the difference by assigning the later chapters to a different time, and thus to a different historical setting. See LaSor, 491–93; Archer, 425–30.

D. It is one of the longest of the minor prophets (both Hosea and Zechariah have 14 chapters).

HISTORICAL SETTING

A. Zechariah has the same historical background as Haggai. Both prophets had as their prime mission to motivate the returned exiles to complete the rebuilding of the temple. (See Ezra 5:1; 6:14.)

B. The Jews had returned about 538 BC, had laid the foundation of the temple about 536 BC, but had stopped building because of opposition. At the urging of the prophets, with the blessing of the Persian rulers, they began again about 520 BC and finally completed the work about 516 BC. (Ezra 6:14–15)

B. Thus, Haggai and Zechariah, unlike most of the prophets, were "successful" in their mission (if "success" is measured in terms of "visible results").

OUTLINE

A. Comfort from the Lord's present concern for His people — chapters 1–8.

B. Comfort from the Lord's future victories on behalf of His people — chapters. 9–14.

MESSAGE

A. Haggai and Zechariah went about their task differently. Haggai approached the subject directly using plain language: "It is time to build God's house." Zechariah presented the message more indirectly; by uttering words of comfort (1:13) and using symbolic language he succeeded in encouraging the completion of the temple.

B. The message of chapters 1–8:

1. Zechariah's primary message is contained in several visions:

- A vision of a man on a red horse, with three other horses, which patrolled the earth and saw the nations at rest, 1:8ff: But God is going to cause the temple to be rebuilt
- A vision of horns and four smiths who cast down the horns, 1:18ff: The nations that overcame Judah are to be overcome.
- A vision of a man with a measuring line, 2:1ff: Jerusalem will be inhabited again and God will care for her
- A vision of Joshua in dirty clothes, 3:1: the priesthood will be cleansed, the people will be forgiven, and the land will be prosperous
- A vision of a lampstand of gold, etc., 4:2ff: Zerubbabel will get the job done, and he and Joshua are the Lord's anointed
- A vision of a flying scroll, 5:1ff: sin will be punished
- A vision of an ephah (basket) with iniquity in it, 5:5ff: wickedness will go back to Babylon
- A vision of four chariots who patrol the earth, 6:1ff: God is in control and watches over His people

2. The message as a whole should be considered:

- The temple will be rebuilt
- The nations which destroyed Judah will be destroyed
- Jerusalem will be inhabited again and God will care for her
- The priesthood will be purified
- Sin will be punished
- Wickedness will be sent away
- And God will control all the earth

3. This part of the book also includes other messages:

- The need to repent. 1:3
- Answer to a question about fasting. 7:1ff
- The need to show mercy to others. 7:9–10
- Promise of a glorious future. 8:1ff

C. The message of chapters 9–14:
1. The message of this part of the book is written in something like an apocalyptic style. In this respect, it is like Ezekiel and Daniel.
2. It is obvious that two oracles are included:

- Chapters 9–11
- Chapters 12–14

There is a considerable difference of opinion as to how the oracles should be interpreted.

ZECHARIAH AND THE NEW TESTAMENT

"Some seventy-one quotations of Zechariah appear in the New Testament ... Most are found in Revelation (31 ...) ... Another twenty-seven are found in the Gospels." (LaSor, 499) For example

- 9:9 — Matthew 21:5
- 11:12–13 — Matthew 26:15; 27:9–10
- 13:7 — Matthew 26:31

THE BOOK OF MALACHI

NAME

A. The book is named after its author, the prophet Malachi.

B. Malachi means "My messenger." This may not be a proper name, but most believe that it is.

DATE

A. Various dates have been proposed, although all agree that the book is post-exilic. Two possibilities: 458 BC and 433 BC. See Freeman, *An Introduction to the Old Testament Prophets*, 349–350.

B. It can be said to date to the middle or latter part of the 5th century BC because of the similarity of the problems in Malachi and Nehemiah. Compare (1) Nehemiah 13:23 and Malachi 2:10–16. (2) Nehemiah 13:10–12, 13 and Malachi 1:7ff; 3:8–10. (3) Nehemiah 13:29 and Malachi 2:8.

HISTORICAL SETTING

For the background of the book, see Ezra and Nehemiah.

A. The people returned under Sheshbazzar and Zerubbabel. Ezra 1–6, ca. 538 BC.

B. Ezra led another group to Palestine. Ezra 7–8, ca. 458 BC.

C. Ezra led a reform. Ezra 9–10.

D. Nehemiah came to Jerusalem (with others) and rebuilt the walls of Jerusalem. Nehemiah 1–7, ca. 445 BC.

E. The covenant was renewed with some reforms instituted. Nehemiah 9–10.

F. Nehemiah went to report to the ruler of the empire. When he returned to Palestine, he found it necessary to institute a second reform movement. Nehemiah 11–13, ca. 432 BC.

OUTLINE OF THE BOOK

A. First charge (implied): Israel was denying that God loved them. 1:1–5.

B. Second charge: The priests despised the name of God by offering polluted sacrifices. 1:6–2:9.

C. Third charge: The people had broken their marriage vows. 2:13–16.

D. Fourth charge: Israel had denied that God was just, for He had not punished evil. 2:17–3:5.

E. Fifth charge: Israel was robbing God by withholding tithes and offerings. 3:6–12.

F. Sixth charge: The people spoke against God by saying that there was no reward for obeying Him. 3:13–4:3.

THE PURPOSE(S) OF THE BOOK

A. To correct abuses which had arisen among the returned Jews.

1. These abuses were different from the sins the earlier

prophets condemned. There is, e.g., no condemnation for idolatry.

2. What were those sins?

- A corrupt priesthood.
- Polluted sacrifices.
- A feeling that God no longer cared for them, did not punish evil, did not do justice.
- Broken marriages and marrying the people of the land.
- Failure to give the tithe.

B. To warn of a day of judgment.
C. To promise the coming of a messenger.

OF SPECIAL SIGNIFICANCE

A. Malachi's method of teaching: assertion — objection — rebuttal (or evidence). See Lewis, 83. Called the "dialectic" method.

B. Malachi's teaching regarding marriage: 1:13–16.

C. Malachi's international emphasis: 1:11, 14; 2:9; 3:12.

D. Malachi's use of the expression: "Will a man rob God?" 3:8–12.

E. Malachi's prediction of a "messenger" in 3:1 and of "Elijah the prophet" in 4:5, 6—passages which, according to the New Testament, were fulfilled in John the Baptist.

THE PERIOD BETWEEN THE TESTAMENTS

HISTORICAL DEVELOPMENTS

From ca. 400 BC to the birth of Christ.

A. At the beginning of this period, the Jews were a province of Persia. Persia had been in a contest with Greece for control of Greece. Early in the fifth century BC, the Greeks stopped the Persian advance. But Persia remained the dominant figure in the ANE until the time of Alexander the Great.

B. Alexander the Great conquered all of the old Persian Empire about 330 BC, including Palestine. At that time the Jews became subject to Alexander.

C. When Alexander died, shortly after his brilliant conquests, his kingdom was divided. Ptolemy took Egypt, and for the next hundred years or so the Ptolemies ruled Egypt. Antigonus became ruler of Syria. After he was killed in 301 BC, Seleucus became ruler of Syria. So the Seleucids ruled Syria.

D. Palestine became the battleground between the two powers. From 322 to 198 BC, Palestine was mostly under the Ptolemies. From 198 to 168 BC, Palestine was under the Seleucids. At the end of this time, Antiochus IV (Epiphanes) desecrated the temple and touched off a rebellion by the Jews.

E. The Maccabean War continued from about 168 BC to about 142 BC and gained freedom for the Jews from their Syrian overlords. Under the Hasmoneans, they maintained their freedom, with the aid of the recognition of the ruler of Rome, although there were constant wars within and without the kingdom. In 63 BC, Pompey marched into Palestine and Judea became a part of the Roman province of Syria. It remained in Roman hands at the time of Christ.

RELIGIOUS DEVELOPMENTS

A. The office of the prophet disappeared.

B. The Davidic monarchy disappeared.

C. Priests became political rulers.

D. The various religious and political sects came into being.

E. The books of the Old Testament were completed and collected.

F. The Old Testament was translated into other languages, especially into Greek. The Greek translation, the Septuagint, was made in the third century BC.

G. The Jews were scattered throughout the Empire; some were living in virtually every province and city.

H. Apparently, there was a determined effort on the part of at least some of the Jews to do "mission work"—to make proselytes. Undoubtedly there were many God-fearers and proselytes among the Gentiles.

I. Hebrew was replaced as the spoken language by Aramaic.

J. The "Oral Law" had its beginning.

K. The synagogue began.

L. A greater emphasis began to be placed upon certain laws —especially the food laws, the Sabbath law, and circumcision— which served to distinguish the Jews from the Gentiles.

M. There developed a strong belief in a coming Messiah, coupled with eschatological expectations.

N. Many other (non-canonical) books, of various types, were written.

PART THREE
Bibliography

WORKS CITED

WORKS CITED

Achtemeier, Paul J., ed. *Harper's Bible Dictionary*. San Francisco: Harper and Row, 1985.

Alden, Robert L. *Proverbs — A Commentary on an Ancient Book of Timeless Advice*. Grand Rapids, MI: Baker, 1983.

Allen, Leslie. *1, 2 Chronicles*. The Communicator's Commentary. vol.10. Waco, TX: Word Books, 1987.

Alexander, David, and Pat Alexander, eds. *Eerdmans' Handbook to the Bible*. Grand Rapids, MI: Eerdmans, 1973.

Archer, Gleason L., Jr. *A Survey of Old Testament Introduction*. rev. ed. Chicago: Moody Press, 1974.

Bright, John. *A History of Israel*. 2nd ed. London: SCM Press, 1972.

Crenshaw, James L. *Old Testament Wisdom — An Introduction*. Atlanta: John Knox Press, 1981.

Davis, John D. *A Dictionary of the Bible*. 4th rev. ed. Grand Rapids, MI: Baker, 1958.

Ellison, H. L. *The Message of the Old Testament*. Grand Rapids, MI: Eerdmans, 1969.

Freeman, Hobart E. *An Introduction to the Old Testament*

Prophets. Chicago: Moody Press, 1968.

Halley, Henry H. *Halley's Bible Handbook*. 24th ed. Grand Rapids, MI: Zondervan, 1927, 1959.

Harrison, R. K. *Introduction to the Old Testament*. Grand Rapids, MI: Eerdmans, 1969.

Jerusalem Bible. Reader's ed. Garden City, NY: Doubleday, 1968.

LaSor, William Sanford, David Allan Hubbard, and Frederic Wm. Bush. *Old Testament Survey*. Grand Rapids, MI: Eerdmans, 1982.

Lewis, Jack P. *Historical Backgrounds of Bible History*. Grand Rapids, MI: Baker Books, 1971.

_____. *The Minor Prophets*. Grand Rapids, MI: Baker, 1966.

Lindsell, Harold, ed. *Harper Study Bible*. Revised Standard Version, 1952, 1971.

Mendenhall, George. "Pre-Canonical 'Prophetic' Personages." Unpublished handout. University of Michigan, 1982.

Orr, James, ed. *The International Standard Bible Encyclopedia*. 1915 ed. Wilmington, DE: Associated Publishers and Authors, reprint, n.d.

Payne, J.B. "1, 2 Chronicles." In *Expositor's Bible Commentary*. Frank E. Gaebelein, ed. 12 vols. Grand Rapids, MI: Zondervan, 1988.

Ramm, Bernard L. *The Christian View of Science and Scripture*. Grand Rapids, MI: Eerdmans, 1954.

Roper, David. *A Survey of the Bible Book by Book — Outlines by David Roper*. 2 volumes. n.d.

Schultz, Samuel. "Interpreting the Prophets." In *The Literature and Meaning of Scripture*. Morris Inch and C. Hassell Bullock, eds. Grand Rapids, MI: Baker, 1981.

Willis, John T. *Insights from the Psalms*. Volume 1 of 3. Abilene, TX: Biblical Research Press, 1974.

_____. *My Servants the Prophets*. Volume 1 of 3. Abilene, TX: Biblical Research Press, 1971.

PART FOUR
Appendixes

SURVEY OF APPROACHES TO THE STUDY OF THE OLD TESTAMENT

INTRODUCTION

I. WHY STUDY DIFFERENT APPROACHES TO THE OLD TESTAMENT?

A. *Because they're there!* They exist, and the person who claims to be educated regarding the scriptures needs to be aware of them. Further, he needs to know the vocabulary employed by scholars to understand them.

B. *To see their fallacies.* The unsuspecting student of the Old Testament, who has never been exposed to any approach other than the "naive" approach (see below), may find the works of critics very convincing. A prior consideration of these approaches will help the beginning student become aware of problems within each; this should, in turn, keep him from accepting false or speculative conclusions as if they were the "gospel truth."

C. *To be able to benefit from them.* Though there are problems with most, or all, of the approaches discussed below, frequently scholars who use those approaches provide information that can be helpful to anyone who desires a better understanding of the Old Testament text. To learn something about the approaches will enable the student not only to understand what the scholars say, but also to evaluate it, to separate the good from the bad, and to profit from the good. In addition, some of the techniques used in some of the approaches can be used by believers with profit.

II. HOW SHOULD WE EVALUATE THESE DIFFERENT APPROACHES?

A. Is this method correct in theory? Or is it based on faulty premises? As a hypothesis, is it internally consistent? Is it externally consistent—that is, is it consistent with known facts? Any hypothesis is judged by how well it explains all the facts in the case.

B. Is this method abused or misused in practice? It could conceivably be correct in theory but misused in practice.

C. Does it help accomplish the goals of Old Testament study? If the approach does not help achieve the purposes we have in studying the Old Testament, its value can be questioned.

III. WHAT IS THE GOAL OF OLD TESTAMENT STUDY?

A. To some, the goal seems to be merely an understanding of how the Old Testament came into being.

B. Others would add to that: The goal of Old Testament study is to discover how the Old Testament came into being for the light that this throws on the history of the Jewish people and the development of the Jewish religion.

C. Some conservative (or fundamental) scholars see the primary goal as to understand how the text of the Old Testament reveals Christ and His kingdom.

D. It seems to me the primary goal of Old Testament study should be: To understand the meaning and significance of the Old Testament scriptures. This is similar to one's objective in studying any work of literature.

1. This involves, first, an understanding of the meaning of the text (of any Old Testament book) *in its own context*—to its

author and first readers, and its significance in the history of Israel. This suggests that the Old Testament is a book worthy of study in its own right, not just for the light that it throws on the New Testament.

2. And it involves, second, an understanding of the meaning and significance of those writings for succeeding generations.

IV. WHAT ARE THESE APPROACHES?

A. Each approach will be defined and/or described.

B. An attempt will be made to show how each one works.

C. Arguments for and against the approach will be given.

APPROACHES

I. TEXTUAL CRITICISM.

A. What is it?

The work of determining the Hebrew or Aramaic biblical text in its earliest attested form; that is, the form best supported by Hebrew MSS and ancient versions as evaluated by proven principles. Textual criticism is sometimes called Lower Criticism, in contrast to Higher Criticism, which deals with the date, unity, and authorship of the biblical writings. (*IDB* Supp., 886; see also "Lower Criticism," *IDB* Supp., 558; Archer, 54.)

B. How does it work?

1. Other textual evidence is compared with the Massoretic text to determine the best text.

2. When there are variant readings, certain rules determine which reading is preferred.

C. Evaluation?

1. While there may be questions about how the work is carried on, no one—liberal or conservative—doubts the value of textual criticism.

2. Most Old Testament students (including most preachers)

will never have the tools (or the time) to be textual critics themselves, but they can understand something of the process involved and learn enough to be able to make judgments concerning the relative value of alternate readings of specific passages.

II. PHILOLOGICAL CRITICISM.

A. What is it?

1.

Philological criticism consists mainly of the study of the biblical languages in their widest scope, so that the vocabulary, grammar, and style of the biblical writings can be understood as accurately as possible with the aid not only of other biblical writings but of other writings in the same or cognate languages.

2. It is also called "linguistic criticism." "The linguistic critic studies words and phrases and their relationship to each other." (Carl E. Armerding, *The Old Testament and Criticism*, Grand Rapids: Eerdmans, 1983, 16.)

B. How does it work? The comparison of Hebrew with other Semitic languages—Akkadian, Ugaritic, and Arabic, e.g.—has led to "the suggestion of new meanings for a number of biblical Hebrew words." (Armerding, 16)

C. Evaluation?

1. No one would disagree with the study of the Biblical languages, or cognate languages, to discover the meanings of the words of the Bible.

2. One caution to be observed is that it is often impossible to be certain about meanings derived from other languages.

III. SOURCE CRITICISM.

A. What is it?

1. It is sometimes called "higher criticism" and deals with "questions of the authorship and integrity of the text of Bible books." (Archer, 54)

2. It is sometimes called "literary criticism," but that term is "now considered a more general designation, including source criticism as well as analysis of style and other features." (Archer, 54)

3. It "analyzes texts in order to determine their structure and composition, possible use of sources (oral or written), integrity (whether the text is composite), and style." (*IDB* Supp, 547) Also defined: "the attempt to discover and define the written material on which the different biblical writers drew." Also defined:

> The analysis of the features of a literary piece in order to delineate authorship, historical setting, and compositional character. It is especially concerned to determine whether a document is a unity or composite and, if the latter, the nature of the sources used and the stages of composition. (*IDB* Supp., 838)

4. Chief among the "sources" referred to in "source criticism" are those of the "documentary hypothesis," which applies to the Pentateuch. However, the method is applied to all the books of the Old Testament.

B. How does it work?

1. See *IDB* Supp., 839.

2. The first objective of this analysis is to trace the history of Hebrew literature. See Eissteldt, *IOT*, 6.

3. The development of the literature was related by Wellhausen to the history of the people of Israel.

C. Evaluation?

1. Con:

a. It uses circular reasoning.

b. It is based on guesswork. The uncertainty of the whole process is evident from the different conclusions reached by different scholars.

c. The evidence used to determine various sources can be discounted.

d. As proposed by Wellhausen, it was based on evolutionary assumptions which are no longer accepted.

e. Even after the process has taken place, the student of the Old Testament must still deal with the text as it is; thus the end results may not be very helpful for accomplishing the objective of Bible interpretation.

2. Pro:

a. From the standpoint of importance: Wellhausen's sources are still accepted as the basis for Pentateuchal studies by liberal scholars (and perhaps by others).

b. Not exactly "for" the method: Although this method is usually connected with an anti-supernatural bias, there is no reason why one cannot believe that the Bible was given by inspiration and still believe that the inspired writer used written sources.

IV. TRADITION CRITICISM, or TRADITION HISTORY, or TRADITIO-HISTORICAL CRITICISM.

A. What is it?

1. *Eerdmans' Handbook*: "Tradition criticism attempts to trace the development of a biblical story or tradition from the time it was first told to the time it was written down." (183.)

2. It is the "study of the history of oral traditions during the period of their transmission." (Richard N. Soulen, *Handbook of Biblical Criticism*, 2nd ed. 200)

B. How does it work?

1. Tradition criticism accepts, for example, the idea that the story of Abraham went through various changes as it was told and retold; "tradition criticism tries to pin-point and explain such changes." (*Eerdmans'*, 183)

2. The focus of tradition criticism is

> "in the main ... the history of on particular oral forms but on certain ideas, themes, or oral traditions ... Sometimes this excludes compositional stages, but more often it includes the

reconstruction of the whole history of a literary unit from its hypothetical origin and development in its oral stage to its composition and final redaction in literary form. So-called "streams of tradition" also come under investigation, that is, the socio-religious milieu of the traditionists (e.g., prophetic and priestly circles) which gave shape and significance to certain bodies of tradition such as the festival rites accompanying the annual renewal of the divine covenant. Considerable conjecture has also been given to the geographical site of origin for these various traditions, such as Shechem, Jerusalem, Bethel, etc. Other tradition historians focus not on specific units of Scripture or motifs, and their development. (Soulen, 200–201)

C. Evaluation? The results "are open to question and must be treated with caution." (Soulen, 200–201)
V. REDACTION CRITICISM.
A. What is it?
1.

The task of redaction criticism is to determine how the editor (redactor) of a biblical book utilized his sources, what he omitted and what he added and what his particular bias was. (*Eerdmans'*, 183)

2. Soulen: It seeks

to lay bare the theological perspectives of a Biblical writer by analyzing the editorial (redactional) and compositional techniques and interpretations employed by him in shaping and framing the written and/or oral traditions at hand (see Luke 1:1–4). (165)

It

functions ... only where identifiable sources are present within a composition such as the Gospels and the book of Acts in the NT or Deuteronomy and Judges in the Old Testament. (Soulen, 165)

3. It has been applied mainly to the New Testament, and especially to the study of the Synoptic gospels. (See Norman Perrin, *What Is Redaction Criticism?*)
4. However, it

is now widely practiced by Old Testament scholars, for example, in the study of the Deuteronomistic History in Joshua through Kings ... and also in the prophetic books .... The aim of redaction criticism is to discern the hand of the final writer or editor (redactor) in single books, or in a series of books, by distinguishing how the final framing stage of composition has arranged earlier materials and added interpretive cues for the reader. In this way one can see how the entire composition was intended to be read, even though much of the content derived from earlier writers with differing points of view. (Norman K. Gottwald, *The Hebrew Bible: A Socio-Literary Introduction*, Philadelphia: Fortress Press, 1985, 23)

B. How does it work? It asks such questions as:

Why does Luke alter the Markan tradition concerning John the Baptist as Elijah? ... Why does he have Satan present at the beginning and end of Jesus' ministry and not during it? ... Why does he restrict the appearances of the risen Lord to Jerusalem and its environs? (Gottwald, 165)

C. Evaluation?
1. Con: "Only when the critic has access to all the sources which were at the disposal of the editor can his findings be

absolutely certain." (*Eerdmans'*, 183.) When the sources can only be guessed at, the work of the redactor becomes even more a matter of guesswork.

2. Pro: If sources could have been used by an inspired writer, then that writer becomes, in a sense, a(an) (inspired) redactor. The kinds of questions that are asked by the method then become legitimate questions.

VI. FORM CRITICISM.

A. What is it? "The form critic is concerned with the oral or preliterary history of a text." (Armerding, p. 17) Its purpose is "to relate the texts before us to the living people and institutions of ancient Israel." (Gene Tucker, *Form Criticism of the Old Testament*, p. xi, cited by Armerding, 17–18) This "presupposes that many texts originally arose in a setting other than the obvious context of the passage or book, and that the effort to trace the saying or section backward in time is both possible and profitable."

B. How does it work?

1. "It attempts to determine the extent of the original oral or written units of material, as the Song of Deborah in Judges 5 or the parable of the Prodigal Son. ...

2. "The form-critical method tries to analyze the type (*German-Gattung*) of literature represented by each unit. ...

3. "Form-criticism seeks to determine the situation or setting in life (*German—Sitz im Leben*) in which an event occurred or to which a literary or oral communication type belongs. For example, a lament belongs to a funeral situation. ...

4. "The form-critical approach attempts to explain how the various units have been arranged or put together. ...

5. "The form-critical approach seeks to reconstruct the growth or development of a type or unit or complex or book from its origin to its present final form in the Old Testament ..." (John Willis, "Form Criticism and Old Testament Study," *Restoration Quarterly* 15 (1972), 3–5)

C. Evaluation?

1. Pro: It serves as a helpful reminder that some (if not most) of the Old Testament had (or may have had) a preliterary existence. Its attention to "types" of literature should also remind us that not all of the Old Testament belongs to the same genre of literature and that this should be taken into consideration when we interpret the scripture. ... To seek the "setting in life" of a passage may help us understand it; this method has been helpful in the study of the Psalms.

2. Con:

a. There is a tendency to break down every larger passage into very small units as if ancient man were incapable of preaching long sermons or of writing anything longer than maybe 100 words. "By dealing extensively with individual pericopes and, in general, small blocks of material, they have sometimes neglected to regard biblical books as individual entities." (David Greenwood, "Rhetorical Criticism and Formgeschichte: Some Methodological Considerations," *Journal of Biblical Literature* 89 (1970), 418–419.

b. To attach one type of literature to only one setting in life (*sitz im leben*) is mistaken. (Greenwood, 417–418)

c.

> The study of form should not be divorced from that of content. No author writes without being aware that he must convey meaning and that the meaning is inherent primarily in the content; indeed, it is arguable that, as a general rule, content was *more* important for the sacred writers themselves than form. (Greenwood, 418)

d. Sometimes scholars cannot agree on the original setting for a form. (Greenwood, 418)

e. To base conclusions regarding interpretation on the type

of literature to which a passage supposedly belongs is a questionable procedure.

VII. RHETORICAL CRITICISM.

A. What is it?

1. Rhetoric originally referred to oratory: the study of the available means of persuasion. It is now defined:

1. The study of the elements used in literature and public speaking, such as content, structure, cadence, and style. 2. The art of prose is distinct from that of poetry.

2.

Rhetorical Criticism is a term adopted in 1968 by the late Old Testament scholar James Muilenburg to denote a methodological approach to Scripture designed to supplement that of Form Criticism. Its task, he suggested, is to exhibit the structural patterns employed in the fashioning of a literary unit, whether prose or poetry, and to discern the various devices (such as parallelism, anaphora, epiphora, *inclusio*, etc.) by which the predictions of the composition are formulated and ordered into a unified whole ("Form Criticism and Beyond," *Journal Biblical Literature* 88 [March 1969], 1–18). (Soulen, 169)

Some scholars see this as a part of Form Criticism and say that it does not warrant a separate designation. (Soulen, 169)

B. How does it work?

1. "The first concern of the rhetorical critic ... is to define the limits of the literary unit." (Greenwood, 423)

2. "The second concern of the rhetorical critic is to analyse the structure of biblical compositions." (Greenwood, 423) This would include discerning "the configuration of its component parts, noting the different rhetorical devices that it contains." (Greenwood, 418)

C. Evaluation?

1. Pro: To deal with the text as it is and to note the rhetorical devices used in the text is a strength.

2. Con:

(a) Rhetorical criticism may employ such an esoteric vocabulary that it is useless for the average student of the Old Testament.

(b) It may also, as in the case of form criticism, deal with such small portions of text that the person who uses it fails to see the overall picture of the book or the larger context.

(c) The aim of techniques for study should be to reach an understanding of the meaning of the passage to the first readers, not just to describe the methods used to present the message.

VIII. STRUCTURALISM.

A. What is it?

> Building on certain theories of linguistics, structural analysis looks at the finished text as a whole to discover beneath its surface the "deep" structures in the society or author that not only shape the text but are embodied within it. (Armerding, 18)

"The structural analyst also works with structures operating in the readers and in their views of reality." (Armerding, 18)

B. How does it work?

1. Structures

> may be traced in groups or "sets" of similar texts, such as in parables or miracle narratives. There is a frequent interest in locating the primary functional elements in a story which appear in a fixed set of roles and schematized plots. Structuralism tends to see deep structures in terms of polar categories ("binary oppositions") rooted in basic mental structures that organize great ranges of human experience into such opposites as good/bad, nature/culture, man/woman, life/death,

secular/profane, and having/not having ... (Norman K. Gottwald, *The Hebrew Bible — A Socio/Literary Introduction* (Philadelphia: Fortress Press, 1985), 25)

C. Evaluation?
1. Pro:
a.

That the final form of the text is a more fruitful field for study than the various putative stages of its history is an idea which comes like a breath of fresh air. Believing scholars, certainly no less than their colleagues, must be interested in the mysterious process of communication and language ... this aspect of critical work claims to elucidate the process. (Amerding, 18–19)

b. Structuralism may simply mean the analysis of the structure of a passage. Thus Culley says:

Perceiving structure in texts is an important part of interpretation, and structure in biblical texts needs a more extensive, thorough, and systematic investigation than it has received in the past. (Robert C. Culley, "Structural Analysis: Is it Done with Mirrors?," *Interpretation* 28 [1974], 165)

With this statement, we can heartily agree.
2. Con:
a. The "purest" form of structuralism seeks the "deep structures" of the text which are supposed to underlie the surface meaning and are supposed to reveal something about the human brain (ways of thinking?). That there are such "deep structures" is questionable. Even if there are, one can question what value there is in discovering them.
b. Many structuralists seem to have no use for "the historical and social dimensions of texts." (Gottwald, *Introduction*, 25) "No

doubt structuralism in general ... [exhibits] an antipathy toward history ..." (Robert A. Spivey, "Structuralism and Biblical Studies: The Uninvited Guest," *Interpretation* 28 [1974], 144)
  c. Biblical structuralism

> uses technical jargon, which is particularly confusing because different vocabularies are used by different structuralists, according to which structuralist authority they prefer and in keeping with their own modifications for biblical interpretation. (Gottwald, 25.)

IX. HISTORICAL CRITICISM, or HISTORICAL-CRITICAL METHOD.
  A. What is it?
  1. Historical criticism covers all aspects of history writing. (*Eerdmans'*, 183) Two aspects of it are of "particular concern to biblical studies." (*Eerdmans'*, 183) "First, historical criticism has determined the techniques for dating a document." (*Eerdmans'*, 183) "The second important task of historical criticism is to verify information found in the biblical sources." (*Eerdmans'*, 184)
  2. Armerding: Historical criticism

> constitutes inquiry into whatever local or historical factors may have shaped the biblical message. For many critics of the modern *era*, historical criticism also involves an application of historical criteria to various biblical texts in order to determine their age, sometimes from an understanding of history that is too rigidly evolutionary. (p. 16)

  B. How does it work?
  1. Gottwald describes what he calls the "historical-critical approach to the Hebrew Bible" as follows:

Instead of taking the stated authorship and contents of documents at face value, this method tries to establish the actual origins of the text and to evaluate the probability that events it relates happened in the way described. Evidence for this critical enquiry derives from within the document and from a comparison with other documents from the same period or of the same type. (Gottwald, *Introduction*, 10)

2.

Historical critics believed that a careful study of the Hebrew Bible, using precisely the methods applied in the study of any literary product, would be able to uncover the actual origins and development of Israelite/Jewish religious ideas and practices which had long been hidden behind the compiled form of the Hebrew Bible interpreted as a unified supernatural story. The valid religious truth or 'message' of the Hebrew Bible could only be brought to light when seen as the religion of a particular people at a particular time and place as expressed in these particular writings. (Gottwald, *Introduction*, 11)

3. Under this heading, Gottwald discusses both source criticism and form criticism. (Gottwald, *Introduction*, 11ff.)

4. As is evident from the practices of liberal critics, historical criticism operates on the basis of certain (unstated) assumptions:

a. In all "critical" (meaning having to do with "higher criticism") approaches, there is an effort to be "scientific." In keeping with this aim, if anything supernatural is found in the text, it is assumed that it cannot have occurred.

b. The plain meaning of the story told in the text (especially in the early periods of Hebrew history) is usually rejected (notice the quote from Gottwald: the real story—the "actual origins and development"—have "long been hidden behind the compiled form of the Hebrew Bible," a form which is seen as a "unified supernatural story.")

c. Since the plain meaning is rejected, other meanings are sought. A certain story, it is said, may be included to explain why a place is called by a certain name, or to emphasize the importance of a certain sacred place.

C. Evaluation?

1. Pro: There is certainly value in stressing the historical aspect of the Old Testament. Furthermore, such methods have sometimes tended to confirm the historicity of Biblical events.

2. Con:

(a) The methods of historical criticism are not as exact as its proponents would like to believe, nor are its results as certain.

(b) Frequently, historical criticism is conducted on the basis of false assumptions—an anti-supernatural bias, for example, or preconceived evolutionary ideas.

(c) It appears that many scholars are inconsistent in dealing with historical events recorded in the Old Testament. They seem arbitrarily to reject certain details in the stories while accepting others.

X. "HISTORY OF RELIGIONS" APPROACH OR COMPARATIVE RELIGIOUS CRITICISM.

A. What is it?

1. "Comparative religious research ... begins with an assumption that the religion of the Old Testament is best understood by analogy to ancient religions in general." (Armerding, 16–17)

2. The "history of religions school" is

> the name given to a group of Protestant scholars in Germany who, at the turn of the century, sought to understand the religion of the Old and New Testaments within the context of their historical environment, including the other religions of that time and region. (Soulen, 167–68)

B. How does it work?

1. Sometimes conclusions are reached concerning ancient religions from the study of other peoples, and then the study of Old Testament religion is interpreted to fit the preconceived pattern.

2. The correct method would be to:

(a) study and understand other religions of the ancient Near East in their own context,

(b) study and understand Israelite religion in its context, and

(c) compare and contrast the two, without assuming that similar forms necessarily mean that the religions are basically the same.

C. Evaluation?

1. Con:

a.

> Such a presupposition must be rejected on the basis of an evangelical view of revelation, and many of the conclusions of the comparative religionists will be unacceptable to believing Christians. (Armerding, 17)

b. The problem with comparing Israel's religion with that of others is that the differences are more important than the similarities. Though there are similarities in form, the content is very dissimilar. It may be said that Old Testament religion, more than being influenced by its environment, stood against its environment.

2. Pro:

a. Nevertheless,

> it is apparent that a study of the religious aspects of ancient society will illuminate many practices within the history of Israel. In this sense, comparative religions research becomes a

part of historical criticism and is regularly employed by conservative scholars. (Armerding, 17)

b. Furthermore, one can believe that God could, if He chose, use religious forms that were common in antiquity for the revealed religion of His people.

XI. ARCHAEOLOGICAL STUDY OF THE OLD TESTAMENT.

A. What is it?

1. In one sense, this is not a separate approach. Usually, those who have emphasized applying the results of archaeological research to the Old Testament assume the validity of other methods of criticism—e.g., source criticism and historical criticism.

2. In another sense, it deserves special discussion because it involves a methodology that is different from other approaches (especially from purely literary approaches), and which is adhered to consistently by a group of scholars who are seen as belonging to a special "school" of Old Testament studies.

3. The original leader of this group was William F. Albright, who made valuable contributions to the interpretation of archaeological findings and their application to the study of the Bible. His students include George Ernest Wright, John Bright, George Mendenhall, and David Noel Freedman.

4. Archaeology has been defined as the study of the material remains of antiquity. Biblical archaeology refers to the study of the remains of ancient civilizations anywhere in the area where and during the time when Biblical events occurred.

5. The emphasis of Biblical archaeology is on history: Does the archaeological record confirm or illuminate the historical events recorded in the Bible? Archaeological research is seen as providing a context for the Bible, and the Bible is seen as providing a context for archaeological research (i.e., the record

of events in the Bible may help explain the archaeological record).

B. How does it work?

1. The archaeologist discovers, identifies, records, dates, interprets, and publishes the evidence from a particular site. In doing so, he works as an archaeologist, though his work may be influenced and assisted by a knowledge of Biblical writings concerning the area.

2. The Biblical archaeologist then correlates the archaeologist's findings with other evidence—writings from other peoples, findings from similar archaeological sites, comparative religious studies, the social sciences, and the Bible itself—and tries to reach conclusions concerning Biblical history.

3. He asks and tries to answer such questions as: "Did the conquest really occur? What happened in the conquest? If it did not occur in the way it is described in the Bible, then what did happen? And how can the later tradition which we find preserved in our Bible be explained?"

C. Evaluation?

1. Pro:

a. The emphasis on the Bible as history is a good corrective, not only to the liberals who ignore history and deal only with documents but also to conservatives who sometimes seem to forget that Bible events really happened and who seem to be interested only in the theological meanings or moral lessons to be derived from the texts.

b. While archaeologists have sometimes been mistaken in identifications and have drawn parallels that turned out to be unjustified by the evidence, the result of archaeological research has, generally, been to produce a more conservative attitude towards Biblical events.

c. Archaeology has also aided in the understanding of the culture (the way of life) of people in Bible times.

2. Con:

a. Archaeological evidence provides only a sampling of antiquity. For instance: Only a small percentage of all the remains of antiquity have survived. Only a few of the known archaeological sites have been excavated. Of those which have been excavated only a few have been fully investigated. Of those which have been fully investigated, not many have been fully reported or published. Thus, accidents of survival and excavation and discovery and reporting may contribute to a mistaken understanding of an ancient society.

b. Interpretation of archaeological evidence is difficult. Sometimes the evidence is ambiguous or too scanty. Sometimes the archaeologist's interpretation may reflect his bias.

c. Mistakes have been made by Bible archaeologists—as, e.g., when the walls of Jericho were identified as those which fell down in Joshua's day, and when evidence of the flood was supposedly found in Mesopotamia.

d. Not all archaeological discoveries have confirmed the Biblical record.

e. All of this should lead students to be careful about saying dogmatically that archaeology "proves" something (beyond the shadow of a doubt).

f. Furthermore, the most important Biblical facts are not subject to archaeological proof.

XII. SOCIOLOGICAL INTERPRETATION.

A. What is it?

1. It stresses that knowledge of the social milieu in which the texts of Scripture arose is necessary for any adequate understanding of the texts themselves. (Soulen, 179)

2. One of the chief practitioners of this method is Norman Gottwald. See Gottwald, *The Tribes of Yahweh: A Sociology of the Religion of Liberated Israel. 1250-1050 B.C.E.*

3. It

seeks to understand typical patterns of human relations in their structure and function, both at a given time in history (synchronics) and in their trajectories of change over a specified time span (diachronics). (Soulen, 179)

B. How does it work?
1.

The hypothetically "typical" in collective human behavior is ascertained by comparative study of societies and expressed theoretically in "laws," "regularities," or "tendencies" that attempt to abstract structures and processes of a trans-local and transtemporal character. As a method the SI of Scripture includes all the methods of inquiry proper to the social sciences ... as well as those typical of the humanities ... " (Soulen, 179)

2.

Within the social science paradigm there is broad concurrence that the biblical writings were rooted in interacting groups of people organized in social structures that controlled the chief aspects of public life, such as family, economy, government, law, war, ritual, and religious belief. ... The guiding question for social science approaches becomes, "What social structures and social processes are explicit or implicit in the biblical literature, in the scattered socioeconomic data it contains, in the overtly political history it recounts, and in the religious beliefs and practices it attests?" (Gottwald, *Introduction*, 26)

3.

Sociological exegesis tries to situate a biblical book or subsection in its proper social setting. ... It further attempts to illuminate the text according to its explicit or implied social referents, in a manner similar to historical-critical method's clarification of the political and religious reference points of texts. (Gottwald, 28–29)

C. Evaluation?
1. Pro:
a. It cannot be denied that there were groups in Israel interacting throughout Israel's history—that there was, in effect, a "sociology" of ancient Israel. To ask and discover possible answers to the kinds of questions sociologists pose can help one understand the peoples of the Ancient Near East and thus can help provide an understanding for the context in which the Old Testament was written.
b.

> The paradigm of the Hebrew Bible as a product and reflection of the social world has the advantage of establishing the public and communal character of biblical texts as intelligible creations of a people working out their social conflicts and contradictions in changing systemic contexts. (Gottwald, *Introduction*, 32)

2. Con:
a. There's a danger of applying modern sociological concepts (or concepts having to do with primitive or tribal societies) to Israel when those concepts are not appropriate.
b. There's an even greater danger in assuming that some great organizing sociological or economic principle or law (e.g., Marxism) must be at work in Israel's history, with the result that one bends everything to fit into that principle.
c. Most statements made about the "sociology" of ancient Israel must be considered tentative.
d. Sometimes emphasizing the groups in Israel may cause the student to overlook the role of specific individuals; empha-

sizing the typical may cause them to overlook the atypical which is really more important in explaining Israel.

XIII. THE BIBLE AS LITERATURE.

A. What is it? Gottwald says,

> Within the new literary paradigm for approaching the Hebrew Bible there is substantial agreement that the text as it stands constitutes the proper object of study in that it offers a total, self-contained, literary meaning that need not depend upon analysis of sources, historical commentary, or normative religious interpretations. (Norman K. Gottwald, *The Hebrew Bible: A Socio-Literary Introduction* [Philadelphia: Fortress Press, 1985], 22)

B. How does it work?

1. Literature is regarded as is

> a world all its own. ... Thus, "Who wrote this book, or part of a book, from what sources, in what historical setting, and with what aims?" is for literary critics in the new mode a far less productive series of questions than "What is the distinct structure and style of this writing, or segment of writing, and what meaning does it project from within its own confines as a work of art or as a system of linguistic meanings?" (Gottwald, *The Hebrew Bible*, 23)

2. This kind of criticism

> stresses the distinctiveness of each literary product and seeks to analyze its peculiar conventions of genre, rhetorical devices, metaphor and irony, and the overall resulting unity and effect. (Gottwald, *The Hebrew Bible*, 23)

3.

There is also an explicit interest in comparing and contrasting biblical literature with other literatures on the assumption that all individual texts comprise one vast corpus of literature and share similar creative properties which show patterned variations. (Gottwald, *The Hebrew Bible*, 24)

4. One more recent practitioner of the method is Robert Alter, in *The Art of Biblical Narrative* (New York: Basic Books, 1981).
   a. He says,

By literary analysis I mean the manifold varieties of minutely discriminating attention to the artful language, to the shifting play of ideas, conventions, tone, sound, imagery, syntax, narrative viewpoint, compositional units, and much else; the kind of disciplined attention, in other words, which through a whole spectrum of critical approaches has illuminated, for example, the poetry of Dante, the plays of Shakespeare, the novels of Tolstoy. The general absence of such critical discourse on the Hebrew Bible is all the more perplexing when one recalls that the masterworks of Greek and Latin antiquity have in recent decades enjoyed an abundance of astute literary analysis ... (12–13)

   b. He says that the kind of "excavative scholarship" that has been going on for years (referring, apparently, to source criticism, form criticism, archaeological discoveries, etc.) is valuable (13–14), but not enough. Literary analysis is still needed.
   C. Evaluation?
   1. Pro:
   (a) Because it deals with the "text as it is," the method may be useful.
   (b) Undoubtedly there are stylistic features in the Biblical narratives which are included intentionally by the author to

make his point (to get across God's message) clearer or more emphatic. To see those stylistic features will aid our understanding of the text.

2. Con:

(a) Modern literary rules may be applied, and modern literary devices may be seen in ancient texts, even though they are not really to be found there.

(b) When different literary critics see different meanings in texts (and they do, for instance, in their analyses of Shakespeare), it is difficult to accept the idea that their findings will be more certain with regard to the Old Testament.

(c) To practice this method well would require expertise, not only in the Old Testament but also in literary analysis—something that may not be possible for most students of the Old Testament.

XIV. THE THEOLOGICAL STUDY OF THE OLD TESTAMENT.

A. What is it?

1.

Theological Interpretation may refer either to (a) the purely descriptive task of explaining what the Biblical texts say about God, his nature and/or relation to creation as understood within the context of their original historical setting, or to (b) the essentially prescriptive task of interpreting for contemporary faith what the texts say on these subjects." Richard N. Soulen, *Handbook of Biblical Criticism*, 2nd ed. (Atlanta: John Knox Press, 1981), 197.

2. Such interpretation may "concentrate on describing what the text meant to its original hearers/readers. Here Biblical religion rather than Biblical theology is central ..." Or it may concentrate on "what the text means to contemporary hearers/readers ..." Or it may "equate 'what the text meant' with

'what it means' or ignore the possibility of any difference ... .' Or it may

> deny the possibility of any simple equation of "what it meant" with "what it means" but ... nevertheless seek some meaningful and unifying perspective by which the historical distance (hermeneutical difference) can be overcome. In some instances, "what the text means" becomes, "what it *truly* meant." (Soulen, 197–198)

B. How does it work?

1. Most conservatives who study the theology of the Old Testament start with several convictions:

(a) the Old Testament in its entirety came from God;

(b) God never changes and neither does His revealed doctrine;

(c) God's word never contradicts itself;

(d) the Old Testament, therefore, presents a consistent set of teachings about God; and

(e) if there appear to be differences or contradictions in theology between various parts of the Old Testament, then the texts are simply misunderstood. It is possible, therefore, to reach conclusions inductively about God and related subjects, by gathering all the passages from the Old Testament which speak to those subjects.

2. In contrast, liberals start with the understanding that

(a) Israel's religion passed through various developmental stages throughout its history, and

(b) there is no reason why different parts of the Old Testament (divisions, books, parts of books) may not teach different doctrines. Thus, liberals are likely to see in the Old Testament, not a theology, but *theologies*.

C. Evaluation?

1. Pro:

a. Certainly one purpose of studying the Old Testament is to reach some conclusions about the religion of the Old Testament. Therefore, to seek to understand Old Testament theology is a legitimate aim.

b. How can the theology of the Old Testament be discovered? Three points need to be made:

(1) On few, if any, subjects does the Bible give all the information in one passage. Thus, to get the truth on any one subject, one must study the Bible inductively, by gathering together all the relevant passages on that subject.

(2) One can do this because God does not change, nor has the basic nature of man changed. Thus, in some respects, there is no room for any development in the theology of the Bible. However, God's revelation to, covenants with, and laws for, man have changed. This provides some room for accepting a developmental idea in our understanding of Biblical theology, as God revealed His will to man, not all at once, but gradually.

(3) Furthermore, it must be understood that Israel frequently did not live by nor obey the laws it was given. Thus, its practices do not always provide a good indication of the "ideal" Israelite religion.

2. Con:

a. It might be possible to study the theology of the Old Testament and lose sight of the importance of its history.

b. Studying the theology of the Old Testament can lead to the worst kind of "proof-texting"—taking scriptures out of their context and applying them to subjects with which they have nothing in common, and making them mean something foreign to their own context. To be done legitimately, inductive study requires that each passage used to understand a particular topic first must be understood in its own context.

c. There is also the danger of imposing structure, patterns, preconceived outlines, and neat categories on the text of the Old Testament, rather than letting the text speak for itself.

XV. THE OLD TESTAMENT AS SCRIPTURE: THE "CANONICAL SHAPE" OF THE OLD TESTAMENT.
A. What is it?
1. Armerding defines it as

> a study of the Scriptures in the context of a canonical affirmation of the believing community. That is to say, the most important point about the text may not be its prior history but the theological role played by the text as part of a broader whole in the context of the community which affirmed its normative status. (19)

2.

> The canonical study of the Old Testament shares an interest in common with several of the new literary critical methods in its concern to do justice to the integrity of the text itself apart from diachronistic reconstruction. One thinks of the so-called "newer criticism" of English studies, of various forms of structural analysis, and of rhetorical criticism. Yet the canonical approach differs from a strictly literary approach by interpreting the biblical text in relation to a community of faith and practice for whom it served a particular theological role as possessing divine authority. [Brevard S. Childs, *Introduction to the Old Testament as Scripture*, (Philadelphia: Fortress, 1979), 74]

B. How does it work?
1. "The canonical approach is concerned to understand the nature of the theological shape of the text rather than to recover an original literary or aesthetic unity." (Childs, 74)
2. It concentrates on the final form of the text. Why?
   a. Because "it alone bears witness to the full history of revelation." (Childs, 76)
   b.

Within the Old Testament neither the process of the formation of the literature nor the history of its canonization is assigned an independent integrity. This dimension has often been lost or purposely blurred and is therefore dependent on scholarly reconstruction. The fixing of a canon of scripture implies that the witness to Israel's experience with God lies not in recovering such historical processes, but is testified to in the effect on the biblical text itself. (Childs, 76)

Critical judgment was exercised in the way the earlier stages of the literature were handled.

c.

The final form of the text performs a crucial hermeneutical function in establishing the peculiar profile of a passage. Its shaping provides an order in highlighting certain elements and subordinating others, in drawing features to the foreground and pushing others into the background. (Childs, 76–77)

d. While it is clear that "particular editors, religious groups, and even political parties were involved" in determining the canon,

basic to the canonical process is that those responsible for the actual editing of the text did their best to obscure their own identity. Thus the actual process by which the text was reworked lies in almost total obscurity. (Childs, 78)

3. As an example, in his chapter on Genesis, Childs has three major divisions: "Historical Critical Problems," "The Canonical Shape of Genesis," and "Theological and Hermeneutical Implications." He spends about five or six pages on the "critical problems," without committing himself to any critical position; he spends twelve or thirteen pages on "The Canonical Shape" of

the book; and about two pages on the third division. In the central division, he discusses "The structure of the book," "The canonical function of the promise," "The canonical function of genealogy," and "The shaping of individual sections."

C. Evaluation?

1. Con: The "canonical" approach to the Old Testament has not pleased either liberals or conservatives. To conservatives, its assumption that a long process of development lies behind the present form of the text is objectionable. To liberals, its insistence that the text as it now exists is of primary concern to the scholar is objectionable because it is, at best, ahistorical or antihistorical, and, at worst, a kind of disguised fundamentalism.

2. Pro:

(a) To deal with the text as it is is always a strength.

(b) The function of the Bible passage as scripture—its theological significance—is worthy of consideration, if not the key to the proper understanding of the passage.

(c) There is value in noting that, even if there were stages in the development of the text, it is impossible to reconstruct those stages. It is thought-provoking, to say the least, that the editors would have intentionally blurred the distinctions between various prior sources.

XVI. THE "NAIVE" APPROACH

A. What is it?

1. So-called by the author of this paper, the "naive" approach involves the "naive" acceptance of the Old Testament scriptures as truth inspired by God. (The first definition for "naive" is "marked by unaffected simplicity." The second is "a: deficient in worldly wisdom or informed judgment ..." The first definition is the one that comes closest to the meaning intended in "naive approach.")

2. Gottwald speaks of this as "the confessional religious approach to the Hebrew Bible." (Gottwald, *Introduction*, 8) He says that the Bible "was believed to be the divinely revealed

foundation document" of the faith of both Jews and Christians. (Gottwald, *Introduction*, 9) He adds that to faithful synagogue and church members,

> the Bible has been internalized as a basic part of their religious instruction, so that when their unclouded 'naive' grasp of the Bible confronts scientific methods of biblical study it often becomes a mind-stretching, value-questioning, and soul-searching experience. (Gottwald, *Introduction*, 9–10)

B. How does it work?

1. Those who approach the scriptures in this way take it at face value. If the scriptures say something happened, then it happened.

2. Beyond that, there is a great deal of difference between the way that conservatives (often called "fundamentalists" by liberal scholars) deal with the Old Testament.

C. Evaluation?

1. One is tempted to say that—particularly from a scientific or critical point of view—this approach has nothing to commend it, *except* for the fact that this is the way Jesus, the apostles, and the early church dealt with the Old Testament. That, however, should be enough.

2. Pro:

(a) This approach takes seriously what the Bible says about itself.

(b) There are reasons to accept the Bible as divinely inspired and as historically accurate.

3. Con:

(a) The acceptance of scripture as true does not solve all problems of interpretation. For those who are conservative, there are still a number of ways of understanding the Old Testament.

(b) This is an approach which was immediately rejected by

liberal scholars because it is thought to be uncritical and anti-scientific.

CONCLUSION

I. WHAT SHOULD THE CHRISTIAN STUDENT OF THE OLD TESTAMENT CONCLUDE CONCERNING THESE APPROACHES?

One answer is supplied by Gottwald, who seems to advocate a combined approach, stating that each of the options he has discussed reflects one dimension of the Hebrew Bible. He notes advantages and disadvantages of each of the four ways of looking at the Old Testament:

A.

> The paradigm of the Hebrew Bible as a *religious testimony* has the advantage of having been the controlling conception by which the collection of writings was made as an authoritative body of texts ... as well as the advantage of being the chief way that millions of Jews and Christians view their Tanak or Old Testament. (Gottwald, *Introduction*, 31)

B.

> The paradigm of the the Hebrew Bible as a *historical witness* has the edge attained by an impressive scholarly accomplishment in reconstructing the main outlines of the development of Israelite literature, history, and religion. (Gottwald, *Introduction*, 32)

C.

> The paradigm of the Hebrew Bible as a *literary world* has the advantage of concentration on the accessible form of the

biblical text and does so with the valuable aid of a comparative body of related or contrasted literatures. (Gottwald, *Introduction*, 32)

D.

The paradigm of the Hebrew Bible as a product and reflection of the *social world* has the advantage of establishing the public and communal character of biblical texts as intelligible creations of a people working out their social conflicts and contradictions in changing systemic contexts. (Gottwald, *Introduction*, 32)

II. OTHER CONCLUSIONS ARE POSSIBLE:

A. Although the Bible was inspired by God, it was written down by man, and put into human language, using linguistic forms and devices common to man. Thus, the message is of God, but the means by which the message is conveyed to man is of man. Therefore, any method that helps us understand (a) the human authors and the time and cultures in which they lived and (b) the language and literary devices that God employed in communicating His will to man can be deemed useful.

B. While it is not heretical to believe that sources could have been or were used in the writing of individual books of the Bible, it is largely a waste of time to try to delineate those sources or to seek their history, since (a) we have assurance that the Old Testament in its present form is inspired, and (b) it is impossible to be able to distinguish with certainty between those sources.

C. What we can be sure of is the text itself: it exists. Therefore, any method that helps us understand and appreciate what the text says and means has some value.

D. Since the meaning of the text is what it meant to the writer and the first readers, there is value in seeking to understand the circumstances of the first readers. Any method that helps us understand the world of the people to whom individual books of the Old Testament were written is of value.

E. Those who are interested in really understanding the Old Testament should reject the method of interpretation that finds Christ (in prophecy, type, or allegory) in every verse of the Old Testament, or which considers the "deeper" or "spiritual" meaning of the text to be all-important.

F. We should avoid a "knee-jerk" reaction to liberalism which causes us to reject anything written by a "liberal" just because that scholar is a liberal. We must reject any statement that denies the inspiration of the Scripture; thus, we would do well to be wary of dogmatic statements from liberal scholars about the source or origin of the Scriptures. But sometimes when a "liberal" deals with the text as it is, his analysis can be quite helpful.

G. From what has been said, it should be obvious that a number of different approaches can be profitably utilized in studying the Old Testament. Perhaps the best approach is a combination of approaches.

PREACHING FROM THE OLD TESTAMENT

WHY?

The first thing to be said is that we ought to preach from the Old Testament. This should be evident from the following facts:

A. The Old Testament was given by God and is profitable for our use. (2 Tim 3:16–17)

B. The Old Testament testifies of Christ.

C. New Testament evangelists preached from the Old Testament.

D. The Old Testament was written for us. (Rom 15:4; 1 Cor 10:11)

An added benefit of preaching from the Old Testament is that in the process of doing so—if we do it right—we are teaching the Old Testament to the congregation (preaching also involves teaching). And worthwhile benefits flow from teaching the Old Testament, including the fact that the more your audience knows about the Old Testament, the better they can understand and appreciate your sermons from the New Testament.

HOW: PRELIMINARY STEPS

When you get ready to preach from the Old Testament, how should you go about it? One view is presented by J. A. Ross Mackenzie who cites John Bright as follows:

> There are four general rules of interpretation according to Bright: (1) Old Testament preaching begins with the interpretation of the text; (2) it involves also theological exegesis, that is, it attempts to lay bare the theology that informs the text; (3) it is a proclamation of the word of the Old Testament from the perspective of the New; and (4) it is the communication of the gospel to men of the present day. ["Valiant Against All — From Text to Sermon on I Chronicles 11:22,23," *Interpretation*, 24, citing John Bright, "An Exercise in Hermeneutics," *Interpretation*, XX (1966), 188–210, and John Bright, *The Authority of the Old Testament* (New York: Abingdon, 1967), chap. IV.]

A. Make sure that you interpret the text correctly. (Or perhaps it would be better to say: Make sure you don't interpret it incorrectly.) How can you do this?

(1) In general, apply the same rules of hermeneutics to the Old Testament that you apply to the New. The chief question is: What was the message of the author? How did the first readers understand the passage? *Priority must be given to understanding the passage in its own context.*

(2) When you study and preach on the Old Testament make sure that you keep in mind the differences between the different types of literature found there. In the Old Testament, you will find narratives (stories), poetry (of many different kinds), proverbs, laws, and prophetic writings (again of various kinds). These all present God's truth, but they present it in different ways. For instance, it would be a mistake to preach on one of the proverbs as if it by itself established a law.

(3) As part of your interpretation, you should look at the Old Testament passage from the standpoint of the New Testament. How do New Testament writers/speakers understand this passage? How does the teaching of this passage relate to New Testament teaching? If there seem to be contradictory ideas, how can these be explained?

In that connection, you need to adopt a consistent viewpoint concerning the prophecy and laws of the Old Testament and their application/fulfillment today. (This viewpoint should have internal consistency and should be consistent with what the Bible says about itself.) To reject some idea because it is "found only in the Old Testament" while at the same time accepting another which is "found only in the Old Testament" would be inconsistent.

B. Determine what is the best application of the text for your audience. Remember you are not interested in presenting history or theology or Biblical facts or word studies for their own sake. There has to be some application to your audience. Every sermon must answer the question: "So what?"

HOW: SERMON PREPARATION

I. As you prepare to preach, make sure that your audience understands the original setting and meaning of the passage. You may intend to wander from the text (though it might be questioned whether you should), but you should be honest enough to let your audience know your starting place—what the text refers to or means in its original setting. You always need to take time to speak of the historical setting of the text.

II. Use the Old Testament in the best way possible, while keeping in mind the goal(s) of your ministry and the needs of the people to whom you are speaking. You can use the Old Testament in several different ways in preaching:

A. Probably the best way to use the Old Testament in preaching is to preach expository sermons from it, in which you attempt to explain and expound the passage in its own context and draw applications to modern life that spring naturally from the text. In doing so, we will be using the Old Testament text to teach the same lessons the Old Testament prophets or writers were trying to teach when they wrote the books of the Old Testament. The premise that lies behind this practice is: The Old Testament books were written for God's people. We are God's people today. What God's people needed to hear then, we need to hear today.

B. We can also use the Old Testament to draw the same lessons from it that New Testament preachers drew. If they used an Old Testament passage to prove the divinity of Jesus or to warn the church on the basis of God's dealings with Israel, and we use the same passage in the same way, our lesson should be doubly authoritative.

C. We can also use the Old Testament for examples, illustrations, specific instances, etc.

D. With great care and caution, we can use the Old Testament for allegories or analogies.

[An allegory is a figure of speech; it may be defined as an extended metaphor. It compares two things in detail. To say, "The water of the flood equals baptism" (as the New Testament does) is to use a metaphor—actually, 1 Peter uses a simile. To say, "The water equals baptism, the ark equals the church, the window equals God's word" is to use an allegory. Analogy is a method of proof. It compares two things that are known to be alike in some respect and then argues that they are alike in some other unknown or unstated respect. "A watch is like the universe. We know the watch had an intelligent maker. Therefore, the universe must have had an intelligent maker."]

If the New Testament writers use the Old Testament to

prove something by analogy, or if they draw an allegory from some Old Testament incident, we can confidently make the same use of the Old Testament passage. If they don't, however, we must proceed cautiously in using an Old Testament text as an allegory or an analogy—simply because these methods are so subject to abuse.

HOW: FORM

Some writers on homiletics today say that the form of the sermon should follow the form of the text. In particular, they emphasize that preaching on Old Testament narratives calls for narrative sermons.

HOW: AN EXAMPLE

How would you go about preaching on the creation? Most preachers in our brotherhood probably approach the story of creation in Genesis 1 and 2 for the purpose of contrasting the Biblical account of origins with the evolutionary view of origins. Their main purpose is to argue that the Biblical view is correct, for various reasons. This approach is certainly necessary sometimes.

However, other possibilities exist:

(1) Consider what seems to be important to the writer of Genesis 1 and 2. What is emphasized in the text itself? Your sermon should not be just a presentation of the "facts," or a word study of the passage. But what is the significance of the words, or the "facts"? (E.g., creation is by God [not gods], out of nothing, by a word, orderly and systematic, "good," etc.) And how do the facts have significance for hearers today?

(2) Consider how other Bible writers/speakers approach or refer to or see the significance of the creation. Creation versus evolution is a modern concern, not an ancient one. It might be

better for us to present the significance of creation as it was seen by inspired men.

(3) Creation is used in the Bible as an illustration of the ideal marriage. But since that illustration is used by inspired men, it becomes more than just an illustration; it has the effect of law. Furthermore, we can use the story of the creation of man and woman to help us understand what the ideal home should be.

(4) Creation is used in scripture as an allegory for becoming a Christian. That gives us the right to preach lessons based on that allegory.

HOW: POSSIBILITIES

Many possibilities exist for preaching from the Old Testament:

(1) We can preach on Old Testament books—say, one sermon on each book.

(2) We can preach on Old Testament characters.

(3) We can preach on the main events of the Old Testament.

(4) We can preach on the narratives (stories) of the Old Testament—either (preferably) by presenting the same message they were intended to proclaim, or, with great care, by using them as analogies or allegories for modern days.

(5) We can preach on Old Testament prophecies that are fulfilled in Christ and/or in the church.

(6) We can preach on the Ten Commandments—all are "carried over" into the New Testament except the Sabbath. But we also need to preach on the Sabbath—if for no other reason than to prove that it is not binding on us today (there are positive lessons to learn from the Sabbath, too).

(7) We can preach on morality, by drawing moral lessons from incidents and laws in the Old Testament.

(8) We can preach on the history of redemption as it is revealed in the Old Testament.

(9) We can use Old Testament stories as illustrations of New

Testament principles—e.g., "what a man sows, that shall he reap," "behold, the goodness and severity of God," "the meaning of faith."

ALSO BY CYPRESS PUBLICATIONS

Ecclesiastes: A Document Designed to Disturb by Coy D. Roper

Approaching Christian Scriptures Faithfully: Twenty Attempts by Ed Gallagher

The Christian Life: Chapters for Bible Teachers by Ed Gallagher

Cruciform Christ: 52 Reflections on the Gospel of Mark by Travis Bookout

Imperative: Studies from the Book of James by Ismael Berlanga

Jesus the Christ: Chapters for Bible Teachers by Ed Gallagher

King of Glory: 52 Reflections on the Gospel of John by Travis Bookout

The Magnitude of God: Exploring the Divine by Brian Poe

Rescue: God and Sin in the Old Testament by John F. Wakefield

Romans: A Practical Commentary by Brian Poe

Visions of Restoration: The History of Churches of Christ by John Young

Women in the Shadows by Betty Hamblen

An Imprint of Heritage Christian University Press

To see full catalog of Heritage Christian University Press and its imprint Cypress Publications, visit
www.hcu.edu/publications

www.ingramcontent.com/pod-product-compliance
Lightning Source LLC
Chambersburg PA
CBHW020245010526
44107CB00002B/112